~ *The* ~
PEOPLE SKILLS
OF *J*ESUS

Ancient
Wisdom
for
Modern
Business

WILLIAM BEAUSAY II

OLIVER NELSON

THOMAS NELSON PUBLISHERS
Nashville • Atlanta • London • Vancouver

Published in Nashville, Tennessee, by Thomas Nelson, Inc., Publishers, and distributed in Canada by Word Communications, Ltd., Richmond, British Columbia.

The Bible version used in this publication is THE NEW KING JAMES VERSION. Copyright © 1979, 1980, 1982, Thomas Nelson, Inc., Publishers. Paraphrases of Scripture are the author's.

Library of Congress Cataloging-in-Publication Data

Beausay, William, 1957–
    The people skills of Jesus / William Beausay II.
        p.   cm.
    ISBN 0-7852-7164-3 (hc)
    1. Jesus Christ—Example. 2. Interpersonal relations—Religious aspects—Christianity. I. Title.
    BT304.2.B39   1997
    232.9′03—dc21   97-3897
                                                                             CIP

Printed in the United States of America.

1 2 3 4 5 6 — 02 01 00 99 98 97

Contents

A Quick Thanks

My name alone on this book is misleading. Books are always a team effort, and I want to take a minute to thank all those who had a hand in this project.

First, my publisher friend and mentor Victor Oliver. When Vic rings you with an idea, you take the call! May God's hand continue to rest on you and guide your incredible life.

Thanks to all the wonderful people at Oliver-Nelson, but especially Rose Marie Sroufe and Brian Hampton. You've both endured countless calls, faxes, E-mails, and more on my behalf without ever losing your cheer. Thanks for all your excellent work.

To my dad, Dr. William Beausay, thanks a million. Your insights and wisdom gleaned from a lifetime of studying this unusual man Jesus are forever recorded here. *Papa, je t'aime!*

Special thanks to Dan Schaefer, Hal "Stratocaster" Filliar, and Dale Bar for taking time to exhort, refresh, and encourage me. Thanks as well to Sara A. Fortenberry and Larry Evans and Rosie Best, three people who have certainly propped me up in my times of greatest need.

Then to Kathi, Jake, Jessie, and Zac: Thanks for forgiving me all those "lost moments" when I'd drift away thinking about sentence wording or scramble to capture some quickly fading ember of an idea. Thanks for making me laugh when I was too serious and cry when I was too flip, and for grounding me firmly in what really matters: people. God in all his wild kindness could not have blessed me with a finer family than you. Thank you. I love you.

For more information on Bill Beausay's
- speaking availability
- training workshops
- print, audio, video, and software products

call him at
  (419) 893-1983

or write him at
  P.O. Box 4444
  Maumee, OH 43537

or E-mail him at
  winners@cris.com

All I Really Need to Know I Learned in Sunday School

One of the most delightful books in recent memory is a short collection of stories by Robert Fulghum entitled *All I Really Need to Know I Learned in Kindergarten*. Their view of life from a simpler perspective makes these tales rich and heartwarming. The author gently nudges us off our pedestals of complexity and morose purpose to a lighter, more childlike attitude toward life and its wonders. In short, he encourages us to revive our youthful zest via a return to the simple things.

Jesus delighted in the utter simplicity of his message. By his own admission he wasn't interested in assuaging the intellectual doubts of his critics. His interest was solely in bringing people to a place of simple devotion.

To that end he openly despised the empty theology of the day. The official religious leaders were steeped in traditions and lengthy rituals thought to bring people spiritual wholeness and closeness to God. They were proud of their record of following the impossibly difficult laws. Jesus wasted few words telling them that they were wasting their time.

Jesus kept it simple.

During one particularly intense showdown, Jesus denounced the scribes and Pharisees as "whitewashed tombs which indeed appear beautiful outwardly, but inside are full of dead men's bones and all uncleanness" (Matt. 23:27). On many occasions he proclaimed that their complicated rules would deliver nothing but death and emptiness. He repeatedly urged his followers to seek what brings real personal fulfillment: simple faith.

What works for Jesus works for a classroom, a boardroom, a production floor, even a complicated work culture. Trying to impress others with your high-minded intellect or micromanaged work objectives doesn't necessarily make you more valuable or interpersonally productive. It's an inadequate substitute for what creates real effectiveness: innocent, childlike simplicity.

Your days are packed with people, schedules, deadlines, and events that drag you into a sticky web of complexity. If your goal is to sound good or merely look good to others, then entering that web serves a purpose. But if your goal is to be effective with people and move toward the real heart of success, nothing beats simplicity in thought, word, and deed. Make your words and actions a symphony of simplicity.

Get a Mission

E ven people with little prior exposure to Jesus can describe the essential elements of his life. Ask any five people you know to describe who Jesus was and what he did, and all five responses will essentially match. I can't speak for you, but I'll bet my very own friends know more about *his* mission than they do *mine*.

Jesus knew exactly where he was going. That knowledge profoundly affected the way he handled people. Understanding his raison d'être provides great insight for students of his relational skill.

It seems self-evident to us that any success is the result of planning and persistent effort. It was not always so clear. In Jesus' day life was driven more by survival than higher purpose. The day-to-day priorities of people revolved around meeting simple needs like staying out of the elements and finding something to eat. People worked hard to survive, and they didn't spend much time thinking about goals and time lines.

Into that gritty, black-and-white world came Jesus. He was the living proof that a person possessing a well-honed plan could achieve magnificent results. Was his plan written

Can you state your mission in one sentence?

down? Probably not. Was it listed in a-b-c points? I doubt it. Did Jesus know what he wanted to accomplish? With inspiring accuracy.

The mission was simple and one upon which he prayed, meditated, and spoke constantly. He declared it most eloquently to a gathering of temple leaders when he said, "I have come that they may have life, and that they may have it more abundantly" (John 10:10).

Jesus could explain his mission in a declarative sentence such as this, he could spin a parable about it, and he could even use everyday events for illustration. The mission was so crystallized in his mind that two thousand years later millions of people know what it was. His mission was a success.

We're driven by business plans, obsessed with the newest calendars, and mesmerized by the latest time management tapes. In homage to the gods of efficiency we chase the most dazzling rainbows. Yet few of us can say what we are about in *one simple sentence*.

Do what Jesus did: Know where you're going, and be able to say it in a sentence or two. If you're really serious, don't ever stop talking about it. Spend some time "boiling down" and simplifying your mission, then reboil it on a daily basis. Meditate and focus on it often. Share it with people with whom you have regular contact.

Choose Your Friends
(Vs. Their Choosing You)

A good friend of mine is a successful local television personality. He has recounted many hilarious stories of people trying to befriend him because of his fame and stature. They send him cards and gifts, invite him to parties, treat him to expensive entertainment, and buy him meals.

"People want to be next to the star," he says. "They're hungry people, Bill. They don't care about me; they just want the warmth of the spotlight."

As I think about it now, I bought lunch that day and felt pretty smug when he introduced me to some gawkers as his *friend*! The limelight has a peculiar magnetism.

Jesus had his own groupies. It was an entourage that began forming early in his career. Try as he might to slip about the countryside unnoticed, they followed him and constantly sought his attention. It made his job difficult.

As his reputation and popularity grew, Jesus chose

*Look for several people you
want for friends.*

followers he would later mold into his closest lieutenants. The twelve people did not choose Jesus; Jesus chose them.

Unless you're a movie star or pro athlete, you probably haven't the luxury (or curse) of having throngs of wanna-bes tailing you. But think about this: Jesus could have chosen any one of *thousands* of people, each eager to serve and worship him. But he didn't choose any of them. Rather, he chose people who were not following him.

Think of your own friends. How did you meet them? Did you choose them, or did they choose you? Some of your friends pass through your life like hand-me-down clothes; anyone who wants them can have them. Some friendships are accidental or purely coincidental. Still other friendships develop at work or in social settings, but only because of physical proximity. No real choice is involved. How you acquire friendships determines the extent to which you will open yourself up, receive input, ask for help, and so on.

Have you ever said to yourself, "Now *there's* a person I want as a friend"? That was what Jesus did, and as a result of choosing carefully, he surrounded himself with allies fit for the difficulties of his mission.

Be careful to do the same. In your business life, social contacts, and friendships, be aware of the ones there by accident and the ones you choose. There is a large difference. Make a conscious decision to have at least several people present because you intentionally picked them.

Surround Yourself with People of Variety

*H*omogenized. That word kept coming to me as I sat in a conference luncheon several years ago. There we were, all in matching suits, carrying similar briefcases, talking about the same things, arguing the same arguments, worrying the same worries, chewing our food at the same speed, thinking essentially the same thoughts. We had about as much variety as two hundred gallon-jugs of whole white homogenized milk.

Variety has gone from the *spice* of life to the *despise* of life. Though we may crave the opportunity to be an original, we're under heavy pressure to homogenize ourselves, from what we wear to how we act and speak. If you don't believe it, just try to do something outside the usual bounds of acceptability and see what happens.

This tendency even influences our selection of friends. There are just some people we can't befriend due to their reputation, looks, personal hygiene, or social status. Even if we

---

Seek variety in your personal and professional friendships.

wanted to, we would face crushing pressure to choose differently.

Jesus faced a similar situation. Though he probably felt no pressure to have a swoosh on his sandals or wear a Brooks Brothers robe, he did confront questions about the variety of people following him. Look at the list: a somewhat obnoxious fisherman, two wild brothers whom he nicknamed "the sons of thunder," a tax man, a doctor (doctors were hated then), even a stranger from a neighboring town whom he'd never met! Hardly homogeneous. Yet Jesus was very deliberate in choosing those men. We should understand why.

Israel at the time of Jesus was actually quite cosmopolitan. There were Ethiopians, Egyptians, Greeks, Romans (lots of Romans), Syrians, Samaritans, and Jews. Some of the people were elite: the Junior Leaguers of the day. Others were considered scum. Jesus was well aware that though people vary greatly in social standing, living standards, ethnic traditions, and so on, the qualities of compassion, leadership, and faithfulness can thrive as easily in the rabble as in the respected. In fact, a mix of people gives you the greatest opportunity to be challenged, strengthened, and fulfilled in your relationships.

Rather than always seeking sameness in the friends you choose, perhaps it makes more sense to seek expanded variety. Here is a list for fun: a janitor, a mortician, a politician, a billionaire, a mountain climber, a hunter, a mathematician, an inventor, an animal trainer, an artist, an IRS agent. Let the eyebrows rise! Jesus was onto something you would be wise to try.

Know Your Common History

I once did some consulting for a successful company with a very interesting leader. When I first met the man, he was driving a black Lexus and had all the markings of supersuccess. I soon discovered that his marks of success came with blisters, and he paid for them with sweat.

His story was spellbinding. Just several years earlier he brimmed with new ideas and zest, but was completely broke. The bankers laughed. Investors curled their brows and snickered. His family, in his words, "gave me nothing but a kick in the teeth."

Through a series of extraordinary breaks, the man was able to create a small start-up and gain a toehold in the burgeoning educational software market. By his own admission he lived for a long time on peanut butter sandwiches and popcorn.

Today he is a millionaire. Whenever I hear the name of his company, I don't think of computers; I think of his valiant struggle. I think of peanut butter sandwiches feeding the empty stomach of a faithful man.

> *Knowing your history increases your value.*

The most surprising part of the story is how few of his many employees knew the history! Once I informed them, suddenly the company that issued their checks and the man in the black Lex meant something special. Suddenly he was real. Suddenly he was easier to believe in and follow. The story made the company come to life.

In Jesus' time, family and cultural history were passed to succeeding generations through the oral tradition. People needed to memorize family lineage and history because putting details on paper wasn't an option. Jesus' lineage was Jewish, and he, like other families, could probably recite his lineage back to the great King David and beyond.

Accuracy in public recitation was a prized attribute for a Jewish man. Not only could he accurately recite family trees, but he could, like other rabbinically trained young boys of his time, accurately recite enormous stretches of Old Testament history verbatim. Jesus knew the Torah (the political, spiritual, and family history of the Jewish people contained in the Old Testament books of Moses), the Talmud (a collection of interpretations, opinions, allegories, and parables created and honored by all generations of Jewish scholars to this day), the writings of the prophets, his family legacy, and more. All of that knowledge served him well.

On many occasions Jesus tapped his deeply studied knowledge of history to make his points. So insightful was his grasp of significant past events that even the wise learned men of his day gaped at his knowledge. His studious attention to the facts of the past provided passage to the deepest respect of those around him.

Knowing your collective history is one of the most neglected tubes of organizational glue available today. You need to reapply it. Become familiar with your company's history, your coworkers' stories, your family background, the history of the place where you live. If you don't know these things, ask. All your histories converge to form your organizational identity. Having ready access to them is a valuable human resource.

Be Well Informed

Have you ever been shocked by a statement or comment revealing that someone you haven't much regard for understands much more than he or she admits? This shock can come from a clerical helper, a peer, or the office pariah.

In these situations we're shocked for two reasons. First, we tend to judge people too quickly. We make judgments based upon whether people act as if they have a clue about what's going on. But people without the look of a clue *often have one*.

Second, well-spoken, informed people demand respect. Let's be candid: We're all confused about some things, and we listen closely to people who have what we consider to be superior ideas presented in a thoughtful way.

Israel in the time of Jesus was a web of political and military danger. The occupying Roman army was brutal and merciless, imposing strict rules and demands on the population whom the soldiers were mandated to repress. The government was appointed by Caesar, and most of those chosen ruled with contempt and hatred for the Jewish people. The

> *Jesus kept his finger on the pulse of his world.*

only real leaders among the Jews were the occasional insurrectionists and the temple officials. There was no Bill of Rights for protection, so everybody needed to be well informed in order to stay alive.

Jesus created problems. To the military leaders, he needed to be watched because his followers seemed to be easily led. To the political establishment installed by Rome, he was rumored to be a new king. Having a powerful new ruler on the scene would not wash well with Caesar. To the temple leaders, he was claiming to be God, which was punishable by death. He was also attracting more and more followers, humiliating their own Pharisees in public, and destabilizing the precarious truce they had with the local Roman authorities. Jesus quickly became a marked man.

Jesus didn't retreat in the face of adversity. Rather, he exercised his extensive knowledge of Roman law, local customs, temple politics, and his own mission. His exceptional knowledge of what was going on around him allowed him to teach for three years and create a movement lasting two millennia.

The same advantage goes to the person well informed about her or his career. Get to know and understand the powers who monitor and protect the path forward. Begin to position yourself for success by being well informed and diligent in matters nobody else seems concerned about. An enormous edge awaits the person persistent enough to deepen himself or herself. Success steeply favors informed people.

Know Your Best Quality

Abraham Maslow was one of the pre-eminent psychologists of this century. He made many thoughtful observations, but one is particularly powerful. He described a condition as "the Jonah Complex." In layman's terms, the Jonah Complex is a condition in which people are frightened of their own talent. They deliberately run from it—just as Jonah ran.

Jonah was a man whom God called upon to go to the Asian city of Nineveh to proclaim a better way to live. But he didn't think he could do it, so he turned his back and ran, literally, in the opposite direction. In his attempt to escape his destiny he was swallowed by a large fish. After three days, Jonah cried out for God's help. The fish immediately threw him up, and with a reoriented perspective Jonah headed for Nineveh.

Jesus was arguably one of the most intriguing men who ever lived. He was immensely intelligent, gifted with people, gentle, tough, loving, and powerful. He is very close to defying description. And one more thing: He didn't suffer from the Jonah Complex, though he spoke of Jonah several times.

Come back here, Jonah!

What was he best at? Everything, though he focused on communication and compassion. He made extensive efforts to clearly communicate the love and power of the kingdom of God in his words and in his deeds.

Did Jesus know his best traits? Of course he did. What is interesting, though, is that he made strident efforts to *hide his strengths* behind his message. He wanted to be the transparent delivery vehicle providing hearers with a means to relate directly to God. He didn't use lengthy lectures and lofty lingo to describe his message. Instead he used clever stories and warm actions to point people where he wanted them to look. He made a remarkably selfless presentation of his earthly business.

If you have been on the run from your talent, stop and come back! You have natural-born gifts and strengths to use today. Be about the business of finding out what they are, and when you find them, offer them with gusto. Let your coworkers and friends benefit from the many gifts you have been given.

Everybody has a Nineveh. Your Nineveh could be a coworker who needs input, a partner who needs correction, a client who needs a good word, a child or student who needs extra attention or discipline. When Jonah finally offered the words he was asked to deliver, an entire city changed. A special kind of serendipity awaits those who offer their gifts and abilities despite their personal fears. This is your call: Go to your Nineveh.

Recharge Yourself Daily

For most of his ministry Jesus was surrounded by people. Lots of people. In many instances it was a near circus atmosphere with hundreds of people crowding around. Dawn to dusk. If you're in management, you can relate.

It was exhausting, and Jesus dealt with it proactively.

How? *He recharged himself often.* He had the habit of retreating and being alone daily, sometimes in the morning and sometimes late at night. What he did to prepare is not exactly known, but eyewitnesses report that he would spend time alone with God.

But it was more. Jesus refueled by doing at least three things. First, Jesus prayed intensely. On one occasion, Jesus was brought a child who was reported to be demon possessed. Evidently the disciples had tried to deal with the child and failed. Of course, Jesus did not fail. When he had healed the child, he turned to the disciples and said, "This kind does not go out except by prayer and fasting" (Matt. 17:21).

Second, Jesus taught his nucleus of followers to focus on and deal only with the day's troubles. It was as if he knew that the day's predicaments were enough to require all their

> *He kept going and going and going . . .*

prayerful efforts. We can easily surmise that he spent his quiet time praying for and planning for those people and situations he would likely encounter *that day*.

But the third insight was the real lightning bolt. It was contained in an amazing interaction between Jesus and several persistent critics. He told them that he was powerless by himself and *he could do only what he saw his Father doing*. It was a perplexing statement, and frankly a difficult one to put into a daily planner.

Perhaps you should forget the power naps and begin praying and refocusing your vision in new ways. What might happen if you devoted yourself to recharging by such unconventional means? Follow Jesus' lead: Retreat daily to meditate and refocus and combine it all with prayer. These are tools any high-output professional has good reason to explore.

Read Hearts

Let's do a test: I'll briefly describe two people and ask you some questions about them. Be honest.

Person #1: A ball cap worn sideways, baggy pants, untied high-top basketball shoes, beeper on the hip, and a can of spray paint in one hand. What is this person's gender? Race? Occupation? Where does the person live? What does the person do for fun? What are the future prospects?

Let's try it again. Person #2: Starched white cotton shirt with a multicolored Polo sweater strategically draped over the shoulders, cellular phone in one hand, *Wall Street Journal* in the other, Mont Blanc pen in the pocket. What is this person's gender? Race? Occupation? Where does the person live? Is this a good or a bad person? To which of these two would you most trust your kids?

We make enormous assumptions based on appearances. We then proceed to categorize people using the thinnest justifications. Knowing this about ourselves, we've become masqueraders, obsessively hiding our faults and weaknesses from

---

*Ignore what people display
on the outside.
Rather, look at their hearts.*

one another. To build a relationship, we must pierce all this posturing and style.

Jesus knew how to get beyond appearances. He ignored the external and read people's hearts. He was consistently kind and gentle to people with soft, pliable hearts; he did not even notice external beauty or repulsiveness. Yet he blasted the facade of people preoccupied only with themselves.

Jesus' interactions with the Pharisees illustrated his interest in people's hearts. On the surface the teachers of the Jewish Law were the picture of perfection: They said the right words, obeyed the right laws, and socialized with the right people. Yet where it counted most, their hearts, the Pharisees were as cold as rocks. Jesus was withering in his treatment of those haughty people.

Move to a deeper standard of people reading. Focus on the unseen internal conditions of people rather than the quality of their presentation. Tune your interpersonal stethoscope to what is beating inside. Though some hearts are silent, in others you'll hear the faint ring of a leper's bell pleading for friendship and union. When you hear it, do what Jesus would do.

Let Your "Yes" Be Yes

Illus.   I once learned a powerful lesson on a car lot. I was with a patient salesman who had spent an hour introducing me to new ways to spend my money. I appreciated his effort and skill, but I was noncommittal. I was really smitten with a two-seat, convertible sports car but knew I would never fit a wife, three kids, and a nasty dog in it. I didn't want to make the hard choice, so I politely told him I needed to sleep on it.

He asked me a favor.

"I can take a 'yes,' and I can take a 'no,'" he said, "but a 'maybe' will kill me. Please make a decision."

I knew what he meant. A "yes" or a "no" means you can get on with life, but a "maybe" confuses everything. I said "no" and departed, my heart broken but my wallet and my marriage spared.

If indecisiveness is the bane of progress, determination and certainty are the engines of action. This holds especially

> *Jesus built relationships on simplicity and honesty. Let your "yes" be yes and your "no" be no.*

true in your connections with others. One of the surest ways to weaken relationships is to be vague and lax in conversation. You may muddle through conversations because (1) you're afraid of hurting someone's feelings or (2) you lack clarity of thought. Family members, friends, and coworkers would rather plainly hear your thoughts and wishes.

Jesus was decisive in the way he spoke with people. He used concrete phrases and seemed to know where he was going with each sentence. He disdained tepid comments. He never rambled, second-guessed himself, or spoke frivolously. Each word had value; he offered each one with clear thought and purpose.

This habit is easier to build than you might think. Work toward learning to say "yes" when you mean yes and "no" when you mean no. Doing this increases clarity in the short term, reduces stress in the long term, and eliminates interpersonal confusion. Best of all it moves all your relationships forward on the bases of honesty and simplicity. Though speaking this way may seem undiplomatic at times, it's well worth the risk. Just ask Jesus.

Come to Life!

As a professional speaker, I'm constantly on the hunt for intriguing phrases and comments that will make an audience react. I once made an offhand quip that, to my surprise, prompted people to reach for their notepads. I said, "Most of us have never met a *live* human being."

Most people avoid living. Real life is a risky, painful, scary proposition, far outside the average person's comfort zone. It's much safer to watch others do the lively stuff, then vicariously participate via imagination. We're a nation of viewers, not doers. It's dissatisfying to live by proxy, but most people settle for it.

Jesus encouraged people around him to reach for something riskier. He challenged his friends to live life at the edge, despite the trouble and pain it demanded. He was very clear that living with ferocity was costly. He was well aware of what it would cost him. Yet with gentleness and wisdom he pressed his friends to find their cutting edge.

A good example of that sort of challenge was his Sermon on the Mount. It was very early in his career, and many peo-

---

Most of us don't know any live people. Jesus pressed his friends to come to life.

ple had gathered to hear his words. As was common for him, he spoke directly to his disciples, knowing that the message would be overheard by many hungry souls in the audience.

His challenge was this: *To come to life, with all its risks and trouble, is to invite the blessing of God.* He promised that such a life, though not always pleasant, would be richly rewarding. He went on to encourage his friends to be flavorful like salt, bold like a city sitting high on a hill, and bright like a lamp. Doing that, he assured them, would lead directly to the life God had built them for.

This is a dangerous message. Most people would be incensed if you told them that they needed some life! Yet when Jesus finished, everyone was astonished. An eyewitness reported that he "taught them as one having authority, and not as the scribes" (Matt. 7:29).

Translated: Jesus was a live human being who redrew the goal of effective living. Then he invited his friends to reach for it.

Come Boldly

When I was a kid, I stuttered badly. I actually didn't speak much through my first ten years of life because I hated the ridicule. I wouldn't even say my own name. Go ahead. Try to say "Bill Beausay" while stuttering. You'll sound like a clattering Model T running out of gas. Anyway my parents feared something was badly amiss with poor little Willy, so they attempted to home cure me. I just stammered away. The neighborhood kids roared. The schoolkids imitated me. My brothers and sisters snickered, and I sank lower and lower into the safety of silence.

When I was ten, my folks took new action. They sent me to a nationally renowned stuttering therapist, and two years later I was fluent as a fiddle. Part of my early success was using an array of simple techniques at the very moment I stammered. I remember one in particular because it was fun: When you're going to stutter, *do it as loudly as you can.*

The theory was not complicated: I stuttered in part because I was nervous. Rather than run from the nerves, I was to roar in their faces! When the technique worked, it was

> *Jesus told us to ask for anything . . . boldly.*

great! When it failed, it failed memorably—just as a bad scar is memorable. I would tell you some of the stories, but you would probably cry with laughter.

Jesus loved boldness. Jesus always rewarded people who came boldly to him. Because of the large crowds surrounding him constantly, getting physically close to him took determined effort. He recognized that, and on many occasions he remarked that people's faith, in the form of persistence, healed them.

Boldness often succumbs to diplomacy and safety. Jesus called people who failed to be bold "lukewarm," and he didn't have much nice to say about them. He said God would spit lukewarm people out of his mouth! (Rev. 3:15–16). I get an image of the Gerber baby eating gruel, his little nose crinkled as he chews a lukewarm glob of slop, each meaningless chomp squishing out more than going in. Get the picture?

Many of us have the cruise control of life set disastrously close to lukewarm. The people in Jesus' time must have had the same problem because he spoke of it often. To counter mediocrity, he encouraged his followers to speak loudly, act with decisiveness, come boldly before God asking him for what they wanted, and act forthrightly in faith. We see this theme of boldness everywhere!

Boldness is scary and risky. It's alternately successful and fruitless. Sometimes encouraging and other times embarrassing. It also happens to be the engine of faith. God can move the world with a person willing to engage it, b-b-b-b-but he c-c-c-c-can't d-d-d-d-do much with a w-w-w-w-wimp.

Astonishing Authority

Most people know at least one person to whom everyone listens. Such people enter a room and a new atmosphere enters with them. These people are gifted with magnetism, a remarkable presence and command that attract people. And they aren't grandstanding. Their words are 100 percent USDA Grade A, no Hamburger Helper.

We usually refer to these people as being self-confident. It's strange that though Jesus had this sort of élan, nobody ever referred to him as self-confident. They used other words, the most common being "speaking with astonishing authority." In several places eyewitnesses referred to people being awed at the way he spoke, saying they had never heard anyone with such authority.

This authority business is very interesting. It's very different from self-confidence. Let's draw an important distinction between *authoritarian* and *authoritative*. *Authoritarian* is best demonstrated in the bad boss: intimidating, shouting, embarrassing people publicly, and influencing others with the use of personal brute power and fear. It's power based on self.

> *Jesus was authoritative,*
> *not authoritarian.*

Jesus was not that way. He spoke with an *astonishing authority:* warmth, perceptiveness, intelligence, coherence, and a piercing delivery based upon a bold message. Get the subtle connection: power based not upon himself but upon a higher source.

You can speak with authority too. Jesus gave hint after clue about where he found such authority. It always involved practicing a faith in something much larger than himself. As an example, Jesus constantly pointed not at his impressive personal track record of success but at his mission. It appears that a key to creating personal authority is being centered and fueled by a specific mission. If your current mission fails to do this, reexamine it.

Root yourself in your mission, whether at work or at home. With the innocence of a child let that mission rule you and guide you. It's the short route to authoritative living.

As Comfortable in Battle
as in Bed

One of America's greatest wartime heroes was a Confederate general by the name of Thomas Jonathan Jackson. General "Stonewall" Jackson. He got his nickname because he was a devastating fighter, impenetrable as a stone wall. He was completely fearless, far too deep and masterful to be showy like the other generals. He felt not a tickle of fear, even in the chaos and terror of war.

His oblivion to danger drew the attention of many. Shortly after the Battle of Manassas a newspaperman asked about the source of his unusual bravery. He replied this way: "My religious belief teaches me to feel as safe in battle as I feel in bed. God knows the time for my death; I do not concern myself about that but to always be ready no matter where it

> *Jesus comfortably roamed the entire spectrum of human experience from the comfort of sleep to the assurance of faith.*

should overtake me. That is the way all men and women should live, then all would be equally brave."

By today's standards of faith we can only marvel at such courage. The man actually believed what he said he believed, and he was perfectly willing to live it out, come what may.

Jesus was as comfortable in battle as in bed. One time he and his disciples were at sea in a small boat when the weather turned vile. Jesus was sleeping quietly in the back. The disciples became so afraid that they went screaming to Jesus, "Save us! Save us! We're going to drown!"

Jesus woke up, looked at them, and asked, "Why are you so afraid? You have so little faith." Then he rose and shouted at the wind and waves. And they quieted.

Humble service was as easy for Jesus as weather control or a tête-à-tête debate with those empowered to kill him. He backed down from neither of the challenges. He is the foremost example of what happens in the lives of people who act upon faith.

Faith can catalyze unusual abilities in your life. It creates action. It creates heroism. It creates imagination and resourcefulness. Faith makes you comfortable in a broad spectrum of frightening experiences. Faith creates the potential to do the impossible.

Today you face a battlefield in some arena of your life. Jesus would urge you to enter it with the faith and surety of someone who already knows the outcome. Jesus would certainly urge you to have both complete faith and perfect comfort.

Finding the Handles

When it comes to connecting with people, one fact about Jesus flags us down: He never treated any two people the same. Every contact was unique and potent. He seemed to understand how to find people's "handles" and how to grip them. Either he knew what other people's handles were, or he was steadfastly in search of some way to connect.

To do this Jesus skillfully utilized something they were already doing as a bridge to make a connection. For example, to Peter and Andrew, the fishermen, he said, "Follow Me, and I will make you fishers of men" (Matt. 4:19). To the half-breed Samaritan woman dipping water at the well, he said, "Whoever drinks of this water will thirst again, but whoever drinks of the water that I shall give him will never thirst" (John 4:13–14). And to the gentle people of the countryside, he said, "Blessed are the peacemakers" (Matt. 5:9).

Finding people's handles is no more difficult than watching what people are doing, then talking about it. Be on the lookout for opportunities to bridge to others by using the incredible array of events *they're* involved with every moment.

Jesus found ways to connect with people.

If they look exhausted, talk about fatigue and offer them rest. If they seem upbeat, talk about how excitement improves the atmosphere. If they're involved in a scut project, talk about rising above nasty work. Whatever people are doing *right now* is a conduit for communication and influence.

You might even decide to go a step farther. Ask people what their handles are. There is no rule that says you cannot ask people what motivates them or inspires them, just as there is no rule stopping you from offering motivation and inspiration. These are basic skills of great handle finders.

Don't Spin Your Interactions

I n our image-oriented world, spin control is an important business. Spin control is a process whereby people put the best spin, or interpretation, on problems or events. Spin doctors aren't rap singers; spin doctors are highly gifted people paid huge salaries to massage the media, explain away conflicts, troubles, and embarrassments, and generally create squeaky-clean images. We can't really call them liars because in most cases they don't outright lie; they just tell us what to believe, and we do. They're very effective.

Many of us practice spin control in our lives. We use our tongues more to conceal the truth than to reveal it. Without making up outright fabrications, we cast ourselves in the best possible light. We pad our accomplishments and use plenty of rouge and eyeliner on our problems. That is especially true at work where we can be led to believe that appearances matter more than reality. Interpersonal deception is expected, and image management is a constant. We're very good at spin control.

Spin is necessary because many of us aren't comfortable with truth. We feel that some truths (about ourselves) are

---

Jesus urged us to come clean.

shameful or at least worth covering. Thus we filter, gloss, and paint over realities that expose or potentially damage us.

By his example, Jesus eschewed spinning. His style was stripped down and direct. He didn't adorn his conversations with words intended to deceive or misdirect. He didn't exaggerate facts. His consistency between conversations was never questioned. Though he was clearly attempting to sway his listeners, he preferred to tell the truth as it was rather than spin it for each of his varying audiences.

He did that from the beginning. When he first started his ministry, he was teaching in the local synagogue. After reading an Old Testament prophecy of Isaiah predicting the arrival of the Messiah, he proclaimed, "Today this Scripture is fulfilled in your hearing" (Luke 4:21). No fancy wordplay. No ad campaigns. No consultants. No damage control. It was just Jesus doing what he does best: speaking simple and straight.

In following Jesus' pattern, urge people at work and home to come clean and talk straight. Doing this requires that each person mature as an adult. Drop the spin and fakery, and get comfortable with honesty and clarity. Expect to feel threatened. Honesty is excruciating at first. But you get used to it. In the long term you operate far better with the shields down, especially at work and at home.

Use Tough Truth

Occasionally I'm tempted to think that Jesus was too honest, too tough. Must he be so demanding? Must he beat up those Pharisees that way? For goodness' sake, come on! Wasn't he trying to attract people? Why blitz them the way he did?

If your business is bringing life (as Jesus' was), you must do what works, not what merely *sounds good*. Using tough truth doesn't sound good to our ears, but it works. Jesus could have schmoozed and flattered his flock, but he knew that would bring only one thing: death. His business was not death, but life. He was looking for something stronger than blowing kisses.

No tool is more superbly designed for high impact than truth. Truth is not designed to be nice but to do the tough work of bringing life. Jesus was the consummate master of speaking the truth in a loving yet effectively blunt way. Even when it bumped his listeners around.

On one occasion, Peter, his loyal and trusted disciple, began to privately scold Jesus for predicting his own death and resurrection. Jesus turned to Peter, his friend, and said, "Get behind Me, Satan! You are an offense to Me" (Matt.

Love loves truth.

16:23). On the surface we would not judge that to be a relationship-enhancing comment.

You must learn one essential life piece from Jesus' willingness to apply tough truth. If you desire to make people better and improve their lot, you must be willing to endure the short-term pain of *telling it* and *hearing it* like it is. Not, mind you, with an ax grinder but with a steely eye focused on personal improvement. Nothing provides more long-term benefit than frankness and candor, ergo, tough truth.

This is especially true for people managing others. You fear candor in many respects because it produces short-term discomfort. Endure it. Before you offer an opinion or judgment today, do a quick gut check to decide what you *really* think. Then quickly and without further thought, speak it. You might be surprised how you sound. In listening, ask those around you for perfect candor, then grit your teeth and bear it. Accept their words knowing that the short-term sting will be replaced with long-term pleasure.

Doing this guarantees a reduction in stress, an increase in productivity, clarity in your communications, and an improved attitude!

◆ 18 ◆

Help Others Understand

O ne of my mentors told me that beyond satisfying the basic physical needs, people are driven to do three things: (1) respond to leadership, (2) seek entertainment, and (3) attempt to make sense out of the world about them.

The last one really stuck with me. Our brains are constantly trying to find meaning, and we can't stop them. Try looking at a road sign without reading it. Try listening to the radio without hearing the meaning of the words. Try tasting a new food without comparing it to something else you have eaten. The brain, by design, wants to identify, categorize, synthesize, and make sense of what it encounters.

Jesus had a very difficult job. By his own admission he was trying to explain truths that would entangle the wisdom of the world's wisest person. He was trying to share truths far more complex than had ever been conceived on earth. To make matters worse, he was speaking to a relatively earthy and fractious populace.

But Jesus was committed to finding effective ways to clearly deliver his message. Once Jesus was trying to explain the unfathomable mystery of the kingdom of God. To make

Jesus grew people by many means.

his point, he created a long string of similes, all beginning, "The kingdom of heaven is like . . . ," a farmer scattering seeds, a farmer planting good seed in his field, a mustard seed planted in a field, yeast used for making bread, treasure that a man finds hidden in a field, a pearl merchant on the lookout for great jewels, a fishing net thrown in the water that catches all kinds of fish, the person who brings out of the storehouse the new teachings with the old. Jesus stopped at nothing to make himself understood.

He vigorously created clarity using other subtle and clever instruction. Jesus walked his message and demonstrated it by his actions, allegories and parables, props, and examples in nature, architecture, and government, and he even preached a tactical sermon or two about it. It's hard to tell what he might have tried had he a multimedia computer and virtual reality.

Jesus never appeared to tire of this, though at times it stretched his creativity. Jesus seemed driven to find ways to help people understand despite their mistakes and inability to grasp it all.

Though the effort will strain your creativity, help coworkers and family members understand you. Write notes to them; say it over and over; make illustrations; tell them your formative stories; point out real-life experiences that illustrate what you are driving at. It's easy to quit on certain people in your life who are dense, prejudiced, sexist, biased, or blind. Jesus' style was to search and experiment and try many approaches to building understanding in others.

Forgive the Weaknesses and Shortcomings of Others

Those of us who must rely on others know this truth: People can be coldly disappointing. They will deceive you, be lazy, ignore deadlines, cheat, lose morale, be inconsistent, and be generally negative. If you know people who never break down, either check them for a halo or give them a raise.

Jesus faced disappointing people, too, and he developed a distinct style of dealing with them. The most memorable example was at the Last Supper immediately prior to his crucifixion. The apostle Peter swore he would never let anything bad happen to Jesus. Jesus stared at him, then proclaimed, "This night, before the rooster crows, you will deny Me three times" (Matt. 26:34). That event happened with aching precision.

Jesus knew exactly where his key players would break down. He had divine foresight and could see when his people were going to mess up.

I'm often grateful I can't do that. I fear I would never trust anybody with anything, choosing instead to handle life myself (which I often end up doing too much of anyway).

> *People make messes.*

That was not Jesus' style. Certain of their impending failure, he consistently let his compatriots go forward. He didn't attempt to fix outcomes, but prepared himself to deal with the inevitable trouble as it unfolded. That approach took massive forgiveness, patience, maturity, and unworldly confidence in the rightness of the mission.

How did he do that? Jesus stood firmly on the knowledge that even though his disciples, family, and friends would certainly fail, nothing could even slightly deflect the power of the coming kingdom. That, my friends, is the power of faith! We should all have a little of it in our daily lives.

You face a choice. The first is to eliminate your friends, coworkers, or employees in advance of their blunders and hire temps. The second is to forgive them their weaknesses and mistakes ahead of time and prepare your grace and confidence in advance. It's really a stark choice but one that makes an enormous difference when someone lets you down.

Somebody will let you down today. Prepare yourself. See if you can look ahead to what will transpire, and try to predict the weak spots, the potential breakdown areas. Prepare your words and actions. Use the "spots" for either corrections or growth.

20

Ugly People

I've read statistic after statistic reporting that Americans think they're overweight. Misjudging our size is easy to do. You can do a fun experiment with yourself by placing two pieces of tape on the wall at what you believe to be the approximate width of your body at its widest point. Then back yourself up between the two markers and measure. Overjudging your size by 15 to 20 percent is common.

To a person with real disabilities, an insignificant obsession such as feeling overweight is absurd, even offensive. I know a young man who was severely burned when he was ten years old. It was a fluky accident involving the incredible stupidity of a neighbor throwing lighter fluid on a barbecue and him simultaneously. He was severely burned over 75 percent of his body. That he lived is a miracle. He understands what it is to be physically marked. His scars make plumpness look like a beauty mark.

In the next paragraph I'm going to say some crass things. My purpose is not to turn your stomach, so please stay with me. This is real life, the kind of thing most of us go out of our way to avoid.

Jesus befriended the "ugly" people.

Jesus came into daily contact with people you could say were truly ugly. Can you imagine the smell of people with leprosy? The Pharisees had strict rules about lepers, and they were not allowed within ten feet of them and one hundred feet on a windy day. Have you ever seen a beggar who could not see, sitting in his own filth for his whole life? Have you ever seen people with severe disabilities up close and personal? How about corpses dead for several days? Have you ever been among a group of four thousand men who only occasionally bathe? Have you ever touched the open sores of a perfect stranger? Have you ever held the hand of a child with an incurable disease?

Welcome to a day in the life of Jesus. It was his style to go to those people! There were no hospitals, no cleansers, no aerosols, no Tide. It was just the ugliness of real life. And he found it in himself to have compassion on those people and love them in spite of themselves.

Though probably nowhere near this bad, most of us need to deal with the everyday ugliness of people. If these people are not physically scarred, they are socially stigmatized and forgotten. Ignoring or outright avoiding these marked people is typical. In many cases it's even encouraged and expected.

If you want to be like Jesus, break the cycle. Talk to the outcasts and befriend the lonely. There are plenty around. Seek them out as you circulate through work, walk your neighborhoods, shop your stores, and follow your kids to soccer games. Find "ugly" people, and give them a moment they'll appreciate.

21

Make People Feel Special

There are many kinds of athletes in the world, and I have consulted with most of them: the famous and the obscure; the rich and the poor; the grateful and the arrogant; the smart and the ignorant; the classy and the disgusting. They all share a common gift of athletic talent to which they have added (to various degrees) hard work and effort.

I learned many things helping the big stars sparkle even brighter. I learned that among our sports heroes are a pantheon of malcontents no more deserving of respect than anyone we could find in the local jail. But I have also found a group of dedicated people who have earned the title of "hero" and deserve our deepest admiration and respect.

What sets these winners apart from others is their ability to make others feel special, even when they're exhausted and defeated. I'll never forget the time I accompanied my dad to summer training camp for the Washington Redskins pro football team. (My father is one of the fathers of professional sports psychology, and I had many close encounters with pro athletes as a kid.)

Jesus focused on individuals.

My hero was an all-pro wide receiver named Charlie Taylor. He was my Shaq, my Greg Norman, my Steffi Graf. I knew him as well as any fan could. I was going to be like Charlie Taylor when I grew up!

Our first encounter was a keeper. We were in the locker room following a particularly hot practice. For those who have never been inside a professional football locker room, it is, well, educational. My guy, Charlie, didn't know me from a tackling dummy, so receiving even a sideways glance from him was a lifetime achievement. Not only did he look at me, but through an odd circumstance, he introduced himself to me and we spoke!

I stuttered quite badly and perhaps he took pity on me. We talked for ten minutes, and he told me I would be great! It was a brief moment, but the afterglow has never left me. I was going to be *great* because Charlie Taylor said so.

The Bible reports that hour after hour, day after day, Jesus tirelessly taught the crowds and answered their many questions. He did it individually, crazy as that sounds. His style was intensely personal and patient. He welcomed people individually, and his warmth radiated deeply.

Be someone's hero today. Perhaps it will be a distraught and frightened student, a harried executive assistant, a forlorn temp. Make someone the focus of your sincere and warm attention. She won't have anyone else focus on her in that way today. Guaranteed. She will feel special and in some small way touched by it. It's a win-win situation.

22

The Home Field Disadvantage

Claude Louis Hector said, "Defend me from my friends. I can defend myself from my enemies."

Nobody can hurt you quite as badly as people who know you best. Have you ever created a great idea or invention, only to have your friends howl with laughter and ridicule? Have you ever harbored a dream, only to endure the humiliation and indignation of your friends' snorts and humphs or worse yet their telling you about "reality"?

This sort of thing occurs often at work. Several years ago I consulted with a management team who desperately needed a means to converse openly without being ridiculed by the boss. I suggested we build or rent a machine that anonymously tallied answers from selected participants (it was about the time television audience polls utilizing the same idea were becoming popular). I suggested we convene a focus group of employees around a conference table to answer questions and gauge the effectiveness of certain solutions being contemplated. It would have generated risk-free, real-time answers and input that could not be retrieved any other way.

The CEO screamed with laughter right in my face!

Ignore your friendly local naysayers.

"In this company," he bellowed, "your *little machine* would cause a riot!"

Some ideas require a champion to push them forward despite intense opposition from people who are supposed to be on your side.

Jesus moved around a lot when he was a kid. He was born and raised briefly in Bethlehem. As a result of being warned to flee by an angel, his dad, Joseph, whisked the family away to Egypt where they spent several years. Wanting to return to Bethlehem, Joseph was instructed once again by an angel not to return there. After some traveling about, his family settled in the Galilean village of Nazareth. Jesus had several brothers and sisters and was raised as a commercial craftsman. He attended the local synagogue, and the Bible reports that everyone was fond of him.

He even taught locally. Yes, the hometown folks and his brothers and sisters listened to him intently. Yes, they liked him. Yes, they thought he was gifted in wisdom. No, they did not believe in him. No, they did not have faith in the things he claimed were true. Yes, some of the leaders were so deeply offended by some of his words that they rose up several times and tried to kill him.

Jesus foresaw all of that. At their lack of acceptance he remarked, "A prophet is not without honor except in his own country and in his own house" (Matt. 13:57).

If you decide to cut and run to the daylight of greatness, don't expect a lot of support from the hometown. Not even your own flesh and blood. Do what Jesus did: Walk right past those people who refuse to see what you see. Remember the saying, "The sky isn't any less blue because a blind man can't see it." Or as Jesus said many times, "Your approval or disapproval means nothing to me."

23

Lose Your Ego

Buckminster Fuller was one of the true geniuses of this century. He invented many things including the geodesic dome (an engineering marvel used to build such things as the World Dome at Disney's EPCOT and the World Pavilion in Montreal) and applied the arcane concept of synergy to architecture. In addition to being a gifted architect, he was a great scientist, thinker, humanitarian, and visionary.

People who knew him best say he possessed one characteristic distinguishing him from the other fertile minds of his day: *He had no ego*. He was completely self-effacing, delighting only in ideas and creativity.

Let me see if I can demonstrate just how rare this is. Today in a casual conversation, contradict something somebody says. Simply disagree. You can see ego displayed in those people who become instantly self-conscious, sullen, and flushed, and they look for all practical purposes as if you called their mom a cow. Egos make people defensive, resistive, defiant, retaliatory.

"Egoless" looks very different. You won't see this trait very often. Egoless people remain calm, poised, curious about

Jesus said, "You think I'm great?"

the nature of your comments, and dedicated to the truth rather than justification of themselves. Egoless people give other people room to speak and express themselves. They don't think too highly of themselves. They actually try to make themselves servants of other people, even strangers. If they do something good, they don't rejoice over their own personal greatness; they rejoice because something good has been done.

Jesus was egoless. When people tried to remind him of what a powerful person he was, he flicked the adulation aside. Self-esteem was not a quality he valued very much. On one occasion a man raced up to him and fell at his feet asking, "Good Teacher, what must I do to inherit eternal life?" Jesus looked at him and said, "Why do you think I'm good? Only God is really good" (Mark 10:18, paraphrase).

Being egoless greases the rails of work and home life. How often has a work project been muddled by the tension of conflicting personalities (egos)? How often has someone been more interested in being right than being successful? How often have silly differences meant the end of a worthwhile effort and the beginning of open hostility? Way too often.

On the flip side, how many successful projects have changed the world because many people *submitted themselves* (lost egos)? You can answer this easily: Think of any outstanding event.

Get efficient. Get smart. Get like Jesus and get rid of your ego. Be quick to open your mind to challenging ideas and slow to ridicule. Be fast to encourage renegade thinkers and slow to laugh at what at first glance seems silly.

24

Extend Common Courtesy

Somebody once remarked that courtesy in the United States begins at the Mason-Dixon line. I'll whistle "Dixie" to that. Once I was doing a weekend retreat in southern Alabama. My kind host had two sons, Will and Andrew, and they all met me at the airport. I was immediately impressed by the two little fellas because of their liveliness and courtesy. Whenever I asked a question, each boy would respond with a throaty "YES, SIR!" or "NO, SIR!" I'm a Yankee so it sounded to my ear like "YES, SUUUUR!" I can still see their angelic little faces smiling at me and shouting those beautiful words.

I'm not used to adults acting with such vigorous respect, much less kids. It communicates something powerful and creates an indelible impression.

I suspect you could thoroughly comb the Bible and not find a single example of Jesus' shouting "YES, SIR!" at his people. However, there are many examples of Jesus' being a very polished, polite human being. He participated regularly in the local synagogues wherever he traveled. Each place had protocols and ritual observances that were not to be violated. He graciously honored the inconvenient requests of Jewish

Jesus redefined best behavior.

religious authorities, mothers and fathers of sick children, and even a Roman army commander. He was a much sought-after dinner guest. He was even invited to parties. Only certain kinds of people are treated with such deference and respect.

So what was he doing? He was trying to be accommodating and, wherever possible, courteous.

Inside our homes and organizations we're recognizing the growing importance of manners. Courtesy can open doors otherwise welded shut. "Thank you," "Please," "May I," "I don't mean to offend you," "I'm sorry"—these are some of the simplest, most effective tools any world mover can possess. Do they always work?

YES, MA'AM!

25

Trivial Worries

Worry is a relative emotion. Its strength entirely depends upon what else is happening in your life. Have you ever been in the midst of a frightful situation only to be overtaken by a larger, darker one? Suddenly the lesser worry completely loses influence over you. Relative to the new, more dire threat, the lesser one disappears.

This response implies that at any moment in time *you must have one dominating worry*. You can't be without it! If one worry disappears, another will queue up and be in the number one position. You'll create it if you must, even if it's a triviality. And you're adept at making relatively small problems feel big.

Think about yourself right now. One dominating worry is casting a long shadow across your life. Can you name it? Is it big? Is it dominating?

Now comes a test. Put yourself in Jesus' position. Relatively speaking, how might you arrange your worrying if you had this day ahead of you: hundreds of people who have traveled miles to see you, each needing personal attention, nothing to eat for breakfast, religious leaders lurking in the

---

Worry about the bigger things.

crowds waiting for you to do something they can use as evidence in an arrest, nothing to eat for the balance of the day, and no place to go home to tonight?

Don't feel bad if you would be overwhelmed; it's a long list of real worries. It's hard to decide which of them is worst. What did Jesus do?

If Jesus worried, his biographers were unaware of it. Rather on several occasions Jesus was overheard encouraging people not to fret about trivial things such as food and clothing, safety and comfort. Focus, he said, on the weightier matters such as love, kindness, respect, long-suffering, and patience.

To the modern ear these don't sound like worries. But Jesus clearly made them high-magnitude concerns. He made them his worries. Upon rearranging his priorities, the trivial matters melted away.

Today you'll face the weight of the world in some aspect of your life. Perhaps it will be a home problem, a hysterical customer or client, an unreasonable boss, a defiant worker, a ridiculous deadline, or worse. Rather than allow yourself to be consumed by worry, address the weightier matters.

Though it may take all your effort, worry about your family, your mission, your long-range plans, and your field-tested ability to survive trouble. If you have the option, worry about something that will take you forward.

26

Don't Complain

From birth, Jesus was a marked man. It began with a personal death threat from the king the day he was born, and it ended with a friend's betrayal, a legal conviction sealed with a resounding public rebuke, torture at the hands of military personnel, and slow death by the most painful and humiliating means devised. Yet not once did he complain.

About a year ago I had some very cool T-shirts made with the words NO EXCUSES! written on the chest. Everybody in the family got one. My motivation was this: As I listened to my family members speak about their failures and frustrations, I heard too much bellyaching and excuse making. We made a pact that if you wore the T-shirt, you weren't allowed to make any excuses about your actions. The pact also permitted anyone in the family to correct any of the so-clothed persons should they wander into pointless excuse making for themselves.

This idea has been a remarkable success. It has also launched many interesting conversations about boldly claiming your errors, fearlessly addressing your weaknesses, and accepting free clothing from Dad.

Jesus kept his complaints private.

Something striking happens when we deprive ourselves of an easy excuse. Whining stops. Letting ourselves off the hook stops. Wasting good energy on intricate explanations stops. We babble less and focus on making headway and doing things right. Does this sound like anyone you know?

Jesus made no excuses and never complained. He was a man of action, and his style was focused on making things happen, not creating polished analyses for why they failed. He was able to be a no excuses–no complaint person because of his faith.

How might this work in your life? Consider spending some time today not looking for trouble, not grousing or complaining about your job or your troubles, not justifying yourself or seeking to hide from responsibility. Rather, assume full responsibility and let it focus and motivate you. How? Do what Jesus did: Become thankful for your trials and difficulties.

What?

It's not that hard. People who have a preset attitude to use their trials to improve life usually do. It's a phenomenal relational ability that sets you apart from everyone.

27

Consorting with Sinners

We have all been on both sides of the pointed finger. We know about being both scourge and saint. We're all guilty and flawed, but that doesn't stop us from judging others, sometimes harshly.

Ask Jesus. He spent lots of time with unsavory folks, and a lot of criticism came his way because he did. He and his followers were called names such as "demon-possessed," "drunkards," and "gluttons." He was questioned ceaselessly about such things as forgiving unfaithful wives, eating with tax collectors and people with leprosy, and generally befriending the scum. And then there was that wine-making incident at the wedding in Cana. Did he have to make *good* wine?

If that wasn't bad enough, he said that those who sinned the most would be the happiest when they were forgiven! The bigger the sin, the bigger the joy. He even suggested that it was impossible to "outsin" his acceptance.

That was illustrated by an incident during dinner at the home of a Pharisee named Simon. A sinful woman came into Simon's home and with her tears washed Jesus' feet. Simon was horrified! She was a *bad* woman.

Spend some time with "bad" folks.

Jesus told him this story: A rich person had lent two people money. To the first person, he lent fifty pieces of silver, and to the other, five hundred. Neither could repay him, so he forgave the debt of both. Who then would love the rich man more?

The Pharisee thought a minute and replied, "Probably the five-hundred-piece person."

"You have answered correctly, Simon," Jesus said. "The person who is forgiven little loves little, and the person forgiven much loves much."

Jesus could really make dinner conversation go quiet.

In all the various places you spend time, remember that "bad" people have value. Who are the "lesser" people circulating through your life daily? Get to know them. They are filled with resources just waiting to be tapped. The top business management gurus have encouraged us with variations on this theme. "Managing by wandering around" and asking low-level employees, "What do you think?" are two popular examples.

Sometimes the baddest are the best. Major talent can easily hide within a life that looks completely unredeemable. Forgive people for where they have ended up, and show them a better way to walk. A huge percentage of them will follow you.

28

Beyond Good Deeds

As a former Boy Scout and Scout leader, I can say with some authority that Jesus was *not* trying to make us into a Scout troop! He wasn't about creating do-gooders; we must understand that to apply his skills.

We're taught as children to do good things. You know the list: Protect the earth by putting garbage into cans, spontaneously help around the house, escort older people across the street, and so on. You can tell it's a great value because you can even put it on a bumper sticker: "Commit random acts of kindness and senseless acts of beauty."

Did you know that Jesus made a whole speech about stretching *beyond* being a Goody Two-shoes? The Pharisees of his day were the elite Eagle Scouts, flawless and spit-shined. Nobody did more good than they. Few drew as much of Jesus' withering wrath either. He warned the people to do good deeds in private, away from public accolades. For instance, when they gave gifts, they were to do so anonymously. Secretly. He said not to even let the left hand know what the right hand did! He encouraged them not to make

> *Jesus went beyond doing good things*
> *for good people.*

showy prayers in public, but to go into a closet and conduct business with God in private.

Jesus understood the hollowness of focusing on doing good deeds without carefully clinging to selflessness in the process. He wanted us to go beyond good deeds done merely for the purpose of self-promotion.

How? At the Last Supper (before Jesus was betrayed) he and the Twelve were preparing to eat. Without fanfare, Jesus stood up, took off his robe, and wrapped a towel around his waist. Taking a basin of water, he began washing the feet of his disciples and drying them with the towel! Why? To set an example of how we should take care of one another. He strongly encouraged the disciples to do for one another what he did for them.

Go out of your way to do deeds for people who cannot possibly repay you, thank you, or even know about you. If you're feeling especially blessed, do this for people who don't even deserve your kindness. Creating a list of undeserving people should be easy. Above all else, remember the revealing remark of Jesus: "If you love only those who love you, what good is that?"

29

Walk with Your Friends

Jesus had a habit vital to understanding his style: He walked and talked a lot. The teach-talk technique was not new. It had, in fact, been practiced under the moniker "the Peripatetic method" in early Greece. But let's face it, when the Son of God put on his walking wheels, things heated up.

I somehow find it impossible to see Jesus sitting yoga-style in a candle-filled temple as devotees fawn at his feet. It's much more believable to imagine him stirring up action as he circulated about. Much of his teaching was done as he walked with his disciples; much of his healing was done as he found people in his travels; much of his personal retreat time was invested walking alone in the wilderness. He accomplished an amazing amount while en route.

Jesus taught many of his best lessons spontaneously. He didn't often wait around for the "right time" to teach and act; rather, he exercised his opportunities as they emerged, whether morning, noon, or late at night. I believe he knew people listen and learn best when their bodies are actively engaged.

Movement is bonding.

Take a walk and think it over. You can easily invite a friend or professional contact to join in exercise or some related physical output. Do this daily. Not only is it good for you, but it provides a unique opportunity for talking, sharing ideas, and interacting at new levels. If there is a special someone with whom you wish to develop a closer tie, cut the chatter and go for a walk. It's what Jesus did.

30

Creating Teamwork

Anyone raised in a family knows the challenge of trying to be happy with people we didn't necessarily choose to be with. The life games we're trying to win with this ad hoc group of brothers, sisters, and parents are serious business. They have highs and lows. They're not always fun; there are precious few tailgate parties, fewer victories, and ever-present challenges.

Jesus built a large, successful team of ordinary players who, much like a family, didn't choose one another. At one point Jesus dispatched seventy-two close followers in two-man teams, assigned to travel about in his name baptizing and performing miracles. They were wildly successful, and God met their every need. It must have been quite a spectacle. Having tried to organize much smaller groups to do lesser deeds, I would rate that as one of Jesus' top ten miracles!

He built such teams (many more spinning off later) starting with a handpicked inner circle. Each man was very different from the other, but they were knit together by one trait: They had teachable hearts. They were open to the message. Despite the typical pecking order arguments and frequent thickheadedness, each had a specific purpose and was

> *Jesus looked for teachability.*

willing to be taught. A leader can quickly create teamwork with teachable people.

What do teachable people look like? They usually ask lots of questions, they're open to correction and input, and they occasionally display a willingness to go the extra mile. When you push them forward, they respond by maintaining their firmness and character, not by turning to Jell-O.

We're all trying to build organizations through people. We need to recruit them, hire and train them, and in the end entrust them to carry forth the plan. Identify your teachable people as early as possible. Make them a focus of your development. Their malleability should thrill you. They are your most valuable success asset.

31

The Gospel According to MasterCard

The advertising pros on Madison Avenue can get you to buy anything. They have razor-honed the science of making you want things you don't need. They understand your weak spots and clearly read your private thoughts. They set traps in your path, then wait with cash registers as you stumble through the checkout. Their skill is impressive; their means irrepressible.

Advertisers are so effective because *we* are so predictable. Since the dawn of time humans have been greedy creatures. It's been a prime cause of war, crime, political instability, and endless other troubles. But we can't stop. Many of us are addicted to the pleasure of things and will stop at little in the effort to gather more stuff. Have you checked out the national credit card debt lately? We have a wild appetite for things.

People were no different two thousand years ago. Once Jesus was approached by a young rich fellow, who asked if the teacher could make his brother divide an inheritance. Jesus rightly asked, "Who made Me a judge or an arbitrator over you?" (Luke 12:14).

> *Think about your people investments.*

Jesus must have spotted the need for a lesson: "Beware of covetousness, for one's life does not consist in the abundance of the things he possesses" (Luke 12:15).

Jesus saw a problem in being consumed by things. To him, it was obvious: "Where your treasure is, there your heart will be also" (Luke 12:34). Jesus had profound reverence for the heart. We can easily understand why he wanted our hearts invested in something worthwhile.

Investing the heart in stuff that molds, rots, rusts, dissolves, and eventually disappears is a cheap way to live. Seek a higher-yield investment, he urged. As we would expect, he chose carefully where he placed his treasure. Any guesses where that might be?

Was his treasure stored up in the rush he received from performing stunning miracles?

No.

Was it bound up in the pride he must have felt giving Pharisees intellectual hernias?

No.

Was it deposited in his status as the Son of God?

No.

How about being able to barefoot water-ski on the Sea of Galilee without a boat?

No.

Jesus' treasure was bound up in the kingdom of God as represented in people. If he worked at your job, he would be personally concerned about the people sitting around you. He would be motivated to do good work, but perhaps more moved by people's stories, conflicts, and pains. He would give the job his best, but give the people his all. You might want to do the same.

32

Test Your Relationships

The thought of intentionally testing our relationships sounds unfair, unwarranted, and unjustified. "You just can't *test* your friends!" we protest. In our culture we value keeping our lives safe and fair. If you test your friends, you might find out things you don't like or, worse yet, get caught!

Let me make a suggestion: If you're serious about your life, listen carefully for a moment and keep an open mind.

Jesus was in a life-and-death dilemma. He knew that most of his closest disciples and followers would be martyred for their faithfulness, and he warned them of it often. Jesus took the certainty of their future very seriously. Knowing that, he would have been irresponsible not to have wrung out his followers just a bit. And he did.

Jesus tested at least three things in many of his relationships: faith, honesty, and reality. There were many examples of each. The most notable example of faith testing occurred about three in the morning out in the middle of the Sea of Galilee. The disciples were bobbing along when out of the mist came Jesus, walking across the water!

Jesus' friends were blowtorch tested.

The disciples flipped; they thought Jesus was a ghost. Jesus, in calming them, beckoned to Peter to step out onto the water with him. Peter did so and quickly sank. But Jesus grabbed him by the arm and pulled him up. Though he flunked that and many other tests of faith, Peter died boldly preaching the kingdom.

The honesty test was evident at the well where Jesus met the Samaritan woman. He asked her to get her husband so that both could hear the good news. She replied that she had no husband. *Jesus knew that ahead of time and commended her on her honesty!* In fact, he informed her that she had five exes and was living, unmarried, with a sixth man! Though she failed the marriage test, she passed the honesty test.

So profound was her astonishment that she ran and told the whole village about what he said. No doubt owing to their great faith, Jesus stayed in that Samaritan village two days ministering and preaching among the people.

A vivid example of testing reality came in the form of a simple question. Often in his ministry Jesus had his disciples circulate among the people, helping in any way they could. The disciples had much one-on-one contact with those who came to see Jesus.

One evening Jesus asked a question: "Who do men say that I, the Son of Man, am?"

They replied, "Some say John the Baptist, some Elijah, and others Jeremiah or one of the prophets."

Then came the haymaker: "Who do you say that I am?" (Matt. 16:13–15).

It was the only question that could test what they really believed. The atmosphere must have been electric that moment.

If Jesus built dynamic relationships asking hard questions like that, maybe you should too. Test those in whom you have placed trust for your career, your business, your family, your life and future. Put your relationships to faith, honesty, and reality tests. Question hard for the purpose of exposing weaknesses and building a stronger base. Make no mistake: This is a difficult thing to do. But remember the old bromide: "What doesn't kill you will make you strong."

33

The Power of a Name

I knew a fellow named Stewart whom we nicknamed "Peewee." What kind of image do you get when you hear the name Peewee? Peewees seem to be expendable, scroungy little people. Nobody wants to go through life like that! Stewart was a great guy, but people become what you call them. No matter how great Stewart ever wanted to be, he would always be that tag we hung on him: a peewee.

One of the more insightful of our mutual friends urged us all to stop calling him Peewee and start calling him by his real name. I'll never forget the day we made the change. Stewart walked taller that day, spoke with greater authority, and in many small ways ceased being a peewee.

Jesus fueled spiraling confidence and boldness in people.

He built people of towering ability and drive. It seems that people who cast their lot with him were indelibly marked for greatness. He never wavered from his commitment that people could be and do more than they ever imagined.

Consider Jesus' interaction with his disciple Simon. Simon had the reputation of being an impulsive, pushy person.

People become what you call them.

He was a professional fisherman. Thus we would expect him to be somewhat indelicate, perhaps uneducated and rough. If the stereotypical grizzled sailor ever lived, it was Simon.

Who would have thought anything great could have become of such a man?

Jesus did.

Simon's life changed immediately after he expressed his deep belief in the reality of Jesus as the Son of God. Jesus gave him a new name and a new destiny. He pointed to Simon and said, "No longer are you Simon. You are now Peter, the Rock, and on this rock I will build my church" (Matt. 16:18, paraphrase).

Imagine Jesus pointing to you and, with authority, renaming you. I wonder what he might call you? What would he see in you that you don't see in yourself? I suspect *whatever* he named you would boldly influence the way you see yourself.

Now think about those you work with, attend class with, or perhaps live next to. What do you see in them that they don't see in themselves? My guess is that you are surrounded by people who feel like peewees and act that way too. What might happen if you began to talk about the strengths and virtues you see in them? How might they change the way they see themselves? How might they change the way they act? How might that change the atmosphere you work in daily?

Take the time to rename those you work with in your career and at home. Give them a new hope and a new image to reach toward.

34

The Element of Surprise

From the beginning of Jesus' ministry to the last breath he drew on earth he never stopped surprising the people around him. He couldn't help it; his words hit with such truth and power. How might you have responded, say, if upon asking Jesus for the route to perfection, he told you to sell everything you have and give the money to the poor? "Surprise" probably fails to describe the experience.

How might you have acted if Jesus came to your neighborhood, and so many kids attacked him that you felt urged to intercede? Then he corrected you, asking you to back off and let them through! Not only that, but he pointed out one of the kids and said that you must become like him to inherit the kingdom of God! Perhaps you can begin to understand why speechlessness was a common reply to his words.

But there were some even bigger surprises. You followed Jesus up to a tomb of a man dead so long that he stank! After a short preamble he called into the tomb and spoke the man's name: Lazarus. To even the most ardent believer, the scene had to seem embarrassing and ridiculous. Then you heard a moan and rustling inside the tomb.

Jesus was a delightful surprise.

Do you remember seeing *The Mummy* for the first time? Boris Karloff all wrapped in strips of cloth, taking one stiff, cracking step after another? My blood froze in my veins. I clearly recall huddling on our couch, eyes bulging like billiard balls. I can in some small way appreciate the surprise that fell upon Jesus' audience that day!

Being a surprise is much easier than you might imagine. What's uncommon are people who try to think in terms of being a surprise. Most of us tromp through life not expecting much and getting less. Surprise these people with kindness, food, help, a smile, a pat on the back, a card, a flower, a note, E-mail, free lunch, a cookie—the list is practically endless. People who are willing to be a delightful surprise are in short supply!

35

Bring Joy

Joy is an old-fashioned word. It has largely evaporated from the vernacular, replaced it seems by its cousin, *happiness*. The two words aren't synonymous. Jesus pointed out that people had a "joy void" in their lives, and his job was to fill it. What was he talking about?

Here is the acid test distinguishing happiness from joy: Happiness is a fleeting feeling dependent upon circumstances; joy is a thorough, deep experience completely detached from ongoing feelings. Its source is much deeper than ongoing conditions. Where happiness tosses and tingles you, joy roots and excites you.

Tell people that you're "happy," and they'll smile with recognition. They'll quietly think to themselves, *Oh, I felt that once too*. But tell people that you're "filled with joy," and they'll blink helplessly and bob their heads up and down like plastic dashboard dogs. "Uh, that's real nice," they'll whisper in bewilderment. Happiness is common, but joy is demonstrably rare.

Few people express deep joy. In our country it's just bad form to look too joyful. People get suspicious. Joy seems

---

Jesus brought a surpassing joy.

incompatible, even contradictory, with seriousness of purpose, which we value highly. We don't see many people modeling the union of the extremes.

Jesus united them. We are at times persuaded to think of him as an overly serious person, arguing with adversaries, speaking in terse, fire-laced bursts. The image of a joyful person seems almost sacrilege.

But the eyewitnesses describe a person silhouetted in joy. Rather than being consumed by duty and solemnity, he had a deeply exciting style. He spoke his joy, and it created an effervescence in the hearts of people. He was like a boat creating eddies of joy as he cruised through the private waters of people's lives.

You'll cruise through many lives today. The swirls and wakes you leave will be whatever you decide. If Jesus were your "skill coach," he would certainly encourage you to stir up some joy by directing people toward hope. Edge your life in the direction of deep joy rather than temporary happiness.

36

Be a Sellout

When I played high school football, our coaches used the term *sell out* to describe a very specific behavior. It had nothing to do with the number of people in a stadium or inventory problems in the cafeteria. I was a mediocre player, and the term meant trouble for me.

To sell out means to voluntarily commit yourself on every play to be a living, bodily sacrifice to the goalpost god. If you're on offense, it means slamming your body into the other guys without caring how badly you get creamed. If you're on defense, it means flinging your body into the path of a team of locomotives despite the high probability of surgery and prosthetic devices. In football, being a living sacrifice is not optional; it's expected.

Which explains my mediocrity. I liked the game, but I couldn't make myself endure the certainty of pain. I just couldn't do it. That meant only one thing: *I'd never even get on the field to try.*

Jesus wanted sellouts. He wanted people to count the cost and decide. It was a "yes" or "no" proposition.

Wanted: People who won't look back.

On one occasion he encountered three men claiming they wanted to follow him. Were they sellouts? The first man said yes. Jesus replied, "I have no home, not even a place to lay my head." You can almost hear Jesus asking, "Are you still sold out?"

To the second man, he used the same words he used to recruit the Twelve when he said, "Follow me." The man agreed but said he needed to go home and deal with his dead father. Jesus informed him that nothing was more important than preaching the kingdom of God. He was asking, "Are you sold out?"

The third man said he would follow, but he wanted to bid his family farewell. Jesus' response was tart and direct: Once you put your hand to the plow, don't look back. Be sold out.

When it comes to achieving any sort of success, someone in your organization must be a sellout. The person must expend time, effort, dreams, talents, and strengths to push the plow forward. This quality separates the player from the fan.

Be that person today. Get on the field and be a player today. Be a sellout *today*.

37

Have a Burð Lite

D ay in, day out, life occasionally becomes a blur for everyone. We have all met the moment when we think, *Okay, now, where was I going?* Life suddenly stops adding up. Where you thought you were going is a mirage. Your days become like the childhood game of saying the words *toy boat* over and over again out loud. It starts out sounding fine, but after about three or four cycles turns into verbal meat loaf.

Jesus was concerned with offering refreshment for this ordinary and expected frustration. To those who stuck with him, it was a special treat. It wasn't beer.

We see a great example of this refreshment after Jesus had spent several particularly grueling days in the towns of northern Galilee. In spite of performing many miracles and doing good works in those places, Jesus received a puzzling rebuke by the Jewish leaders and people. Within his small band of followers morale must have been at an all-time low. They were probably dazed and confused. We can only imagine the boiling frustration Jesus must have felt.

When most people heat up or tire out, they get irrational. They make angry comments and thoughtless remarks to vent

Jesus offered new refreshment.

their exhaustion. Jesus was different; he used his anger to make one of the sweetest offers ever given to humankind.

"Come to Me, all you who labor and are heavy laden, and I will give you rest," he said. "For My yoke is easy and My burden is light" (Matt. 11:28, 30).

Many of us are intense people. We're winners because we know how to "crack the whip" and get things done. Nobody knows this better than our subordinates.

Taking the time to give those people an occasional respite from their yoke and some encouragement in the face of their burdens is a powerful act. This is especially so if like Jesus, you share a burden alongside partners, coworkers, employees, and friends (which you probably do). Today, lighten the load for someone who has been stuck in a hostile Galilean village too long.

38

Keep Some Strength in Reserve

Power is intoxicating. It brings those who imbibe a strong rush of pleasure and a sense of omnipotence. Only people with great inner strength and balance can handle it without being overcome. Only people possessing real authority and self-command can use the power they need and forgo cheap shows of force.

Few would argue that Jesus was a very powerful person. He had to use only a token microwatt of his kilowatt source to do all his earthly deeds. Jesus commanded legions of angels, knew the future, exercised control over death, and had a raft of other abilities. Yet he never showed them much. In fact, he actively tried to avoid what would have been breathtaking demonstrations.

But his power created problems. People were drawn to him for all the wrong reasons. They wanted to see the show. They wanted to see a fight. They wanted dinner. Jesus was well aware of their motives and on several occasions flatly refused to indulge their selfish clamoring.

Sometimes, however, it was unavoidable. Once in the presence of a group of Pharisees he forgave the sins of a man who could not walk. In fielding their insistent complaints

Jesus was discreet in his use of power.

about his authority to forgive sins, he asked, "Which is easier, to say, 'Your sins are forgiven you,' or to say, 'Arise and walk'?" (Matt. 9:5). I think most of us would find it very difficult to tell a disabled person to rise and walk. Though he gallantly tried to avoid a power surge, he issued a sharp command to the man, and the man rose and walked.

The lesson here is straightforward. God has given you many strengths and gifts. Much more perhaps than you know. Use them discreetly and for the purposes of advancing the community of people around you. Don't let your personal position and authority be a bully pulpit for your power. Rather, put your strengths at the disposal of your position for the purposes of advancing others.

39

Be Fond of Children, and Let Them Be Fond of You

Kids are the salt and pepper of life, and few things are as healthy as wanting kids, protecting them, and loving them to death. Literally.

Jesus had many interesting comments and interactions regarding children. He suggested that we be fond of kids for three reasons: (1) Fondness of kids (and their fondness of you) is a measure of emotional and spiritual health, (2) living with childlike wonder and enthusiasm is a magnificent achievement, and (3) the greatest people in the world are a lot like children.

The first two lessons are closely linked. Jesus probably experienced mob scenes with kids more than once. One time it was certainly so raucous that the grumpy disciples tried to brush the rowdies away. Jesus interceded and hailed the kids over. He certainly had a key relational gift that attracts little people to adults to this day: a lively glimmer in his eyes and an open, warm face. I don't mean to be judgmental, but what

> *Childlikeness is a sign of overall health.*

kind of face do you have? Do kids mob you in public or run away screaming?

On one occasion the chief priests of the temple were upset because the children were making up joyful songs about Jesus! Do children make up songs about you? The kids obviously received signals of warmth and acceptance from Jesus. Their attraction to him was certainly an indication of his liveliness and emotional strength.

The last lesson was perhaps his most profound. Jesus hailed a child over in response to one of his most recurring problems: infighting among the disciples over which one was the best. He told them all that unless they became humble like the little child standing in their presence, they would never achieve greatness!

Perhaps there is some sense in replacing the corporate gym with a sandbox. If we are sincerely interested in living a full life, we need to consider the extent to which we have drifted away from childlikeness. Injecting some playfulness into our professional relationships is a vitamin we can no longer avoid.

This is an easy pill to swallow. The energy and freshness of childhood are delightful reprieves from chronic adultism. Besides, as Jesus taught, we'll get farther along the road of life if we step away from the stoicism of adulthood and try to recapture what it means to be childlike, especially in places where children are forbidden (read "careers")!

40

Think on Your Feet

There are several risks in opening your mouth and stating an opinion. Too many people, because they have never learned how to present a coherent and reasoned opinion, are petrified by the risks. Thus they muffle themselves and resort to either truisms or predigested propaganda from whatever source excites them.

Jesus had no such luxury. What he was saying was completely original. What he was presenting flew in the face of all accepted religious doctrine of the day, thus framing the uphill intellectual struggle that would mark his life. He needed to be on his toes at all times. He was hounded by various authorities whose full-time obsession was tripping him up in some way. And their purposes were not academic; they wanted grounds upon which to kill him.

The famed criminal defense attorney Gerry Spence wrote a stimulating and successful book entitled *How to Argue and Win Every Time*. At the very heart of his approach is something so simple that it will surprise you. The key to winning arguments, says Spence, is to find out what it is about your subject that makes you passionate, then present your case

Jesus was never caught flat-footed.

from that perspective. True passion, fueled by what you deeply believe, creates flowing persuasiveness and capability.

Jesus stood and delivered. His words carved with consistency and precision, and never was he at a loss for the right words either with friend or with foe.

What is interesting is that Jesus never spoke about passion. As it turns out he wasn't interested in winning debates; his interest was in influencing people. The most visible proof of this truth is the advice he gave his disciples. He told them not to worry about what they would say in public because God would be there and fill their mouths with the right words.

I heard a quote by filmmaker Woody Allen, who said, "Eighty percent of success is showing up." What is "showing up" in this case? Searching for problems to fix. Asking how you can be of value, even though you may not have any idea. Speaking up when you have a question. Quieting down when your words serve no purpose. Developing ways to be of more value to the organizations of which you're a part. Taking a stand. Taking a risk. Finding a passion.

What is the remaining 20 percent? Open your mouth and trust God.

41

Artfully Evasive

Being evasive sounds so cowardly. Disingenuous. But if we wish to understand Jesus' style, we must consider the many times and reasons Jesus slipped around and sought to make himself unseen.

His evasiveness had purpose. It took two clear forms: (1) physically escaping danger, and (2) not showing that he was the Messiah before the time was right.

We have all experienced seeing someone we wish to avoid, then looking away, slipping in behind the bread rack or belly crawling to the exit. One time I held up a frozen fifteen-pound turkey in front of my face! I must have looked like a body walking around with a turkey head.

There are many reasons for acting this way, but it's usually not because the other person wants to murder you.

Jesus had that problem, however. He never picked fights or looked for trouble, but trouble always found him. In order to preserve his life, he was forced on occasion to duck out. Jesus knew that eventually he would be pushed off the gangplank; that was why he came. *But it would be on his terms as he saw God directing it*. It wasn't that he was protecting his own

---

If you choose to be evasive, know why.

skin; rather, he knew the exact conditions under which he would have the option to offer it.

A more artful-type evasion that we often see is Jesus commanding that people not expose him as the Messiah. We must wonder why. Didn't he come to make himself known?

Yes and no. Jesus was becoming known for the wrong things. Jesus created bumper-to-bumper miracles throughout his days, too many to be recorded. To keep his followers fixed on the message and not on him, he sometimes asked those whom he healed not to talk about what happened.

The relational lessons for us are profound. First, stay alive. It's important for building connections. Second, remember that Jesus' consuming passion was spreading the message. That required a mixture of properly aging his relationships along with making well-timed introductions of new information. In your personal relationships think about what you wish to share and where you want the relationship to grow.

If it's a professional relationship, keep in mind your "swots": *s*trengths, *w*eaknesses, *o*pportunities, and *t*hreats. Make some decisions about what you want from the relationship, and consider what is required to enrich or enliven the relationship.

Then sensitize yourself to timing. It's relational suicide to divulge too much too fast. Ask Jesus. Be alert and mature about when relationships are ready for details, wild ideas, character flaws, and other key elements that affect progressive human connections.

42

Settle Disputes

Our interpersonal troubles may build into anger that scalds us internally. It's like holding a hot bite of food in the mouth too long, then blaming the cook for the blister.

A centerpiece of Jesus' teaching was about managing interpersonal conflicts. I would be misleading you if I suggested that the solutions he offered were easy. They involved one of the most difficult acts in all of human experience: humility.

He had ample opportunity to test it out among his men. They acted at times like a bunch of new corporate employees, all jockeying to be the boss's pet. His advice, intended to stop the elbowing, backbiting, and politicking, was poorly received.

In a seminar I conduct we practice what I call "greasy words." Greasy words are ones that lubricate our relationships, such as, "You mean a lot to me"; "I'm glad we're working together"; "I need to ask your forgiveness"; and so on. These are different from the more common "delubing" words,

---

Jesus used the three hardest words in the language: "I forgive you."

such as, "What a jerk!"; "If I had a dime for every mistake you make"; and "I'm calling my attorney!"

One of the most entertaining greasy phrases is saying, "I'm sorry; I was wrong." It's entertaining because of the way people's faces cringe and twist as they say those words to one another! We're awful at this! It's a supreme (and rare) act of humility for someone to admit being wrong about something.

Jesus suggested that we quickly and humbly fix troubled relationships. It was so vital that at one point he made a startling suggestion. He said that even if his followers were in the middle of worshiping and remembered a wrong they had committed, they were to immediately go away and correct it!

Friction and combustion at work and home are normal. Deal with these troubles quickly, humbly, and without fanfare. Make it your policy to settle work and home disputes posthaste. To prolong it, or worse, to ignore it sets the stage for rumor mills, seething anger that grinds production to a halt, and bitter rivalries that make life miserable.

Spit out hot disputes quickly. And never forget the three hardest words in the human lexicon.

43

Dealing with Deceitful People and Enemies

Twenty-five percent of your acquaintances don't like you and never will. Another 25 percent don't like you, but could be persuaded to like you under the right circumstances. Another 25 percent like you, but could easily be persuaded to dislike you. The last 25 percent like you, and will stand by you no matter what you do."

When I first heard these statistics at a dinner meeting, I was incredulous. Out of curiosity I sat down and compiled a list of people I knew. Next to their names I wrote 1-2-3-4, depending on the type of acquaintance I judged each to be. After the list grew to about fifty, I stopped to check the percentages. I was shocked. Try it.

It will come as no surprise that Jesus was an ace judge of people. Nobody needed to tell him about what lurked deep down. He seemed especially wary of people who offered tempting but empty platitudes. He knew that the scorch of being a true follower would wither them instantly. Those people were deceitful to the extent that they were deceiving themselves.

Jesus dealt directly with his enemies.

Jesus' way of dealing with enemies was, as we might expect, unusual. High school biology taught us all about the fight-or-flight instinct in organisms. All species, when faced with a challenge, either put up their dukes or run away. Jesus pioneered a third: Love your enemies.

How in the world do you do that?

You can follow Jesus' model of dealing with enemies and deceitful people by doing two things. First, be aware of who in your daily cadre is a friend and who is not. Treat everyone as equally as you can, but always be aware of the difference.

Second, be as loving and direct with enemies and deceitful people as possible. In case you need to be warned, this is very hard to do. Don't treat these people meanly; rather, selflessly accept them in the full knowledge that they'll probably never be allies.

Adopting this attitude allows you to be, in Jesus' words, "innocent as a dove and wise as a snake" (Matt. 10:16, paraphrase). It's a productive skill in dealing with difficult people. Don't even be surprised if in some cases your attitude turns them around.

44

Be Occasionally Audacious

Jesus was not averse to making a spectacle of himself. It bordered on audacity. There were several occasions that had we been present, we would have surely disavowed any knowledge of him. Since too many of us are thin-skinned when it comes to public demonstrations of guts, we ought to know where Jesus picked up the idea of being occasionally audacious.

One of Jesus' favorite people was a wild man named John. John was a godly person, a prophet who dressed in weird clothes, lived out in the Judean hills, ate bugs, and baptized people as a public sign that they had turned toward God.

If audacity were a practiced art, the guy would have been Picasso. From his public pulpit, John told people to watch for the Messiah who was near. He told them to be honest, feed the poor, do good work at their jobs, and be content with their pay! He occasionally yelled. He went so far as to call a certain group of them a "brood of vipers!" (Matt. 3:7). Can you imagine the audacity! Can you imagine the nerve!

At one point he publicly chastised Herod, the ruler of Galilee, for marrying his own brother's wife. John paid for that swatch of chutzpah with his head.

Go ahead. Scream it!

Jesus loved boldness born of humble faith. John epitomized that, and there were few who more influenced Jesus in his early years than that audacious man. Though Jesus was a vastly more sophisticated communicator, his adoration of John the Baptist was boundless: "I say to you, among those born of women there has not risen one greater than John" (Matt. 11:11).

A little audacity is a good thing. All of us have at least a glimmer of admiration for those who are comfortable with themselves and bold about it. We all wish for that kind of comfort. Go ahead; show a little of your audacity. Most of your work peers probably don't know the "real you." Show 'em. It's a wonderful exercise in relationship building. Have some fun with it.

45

Pray

Not long ago we took five of our kids' friends to church on Sunday morning. It was the first time one kid had been in a church in years. When we came home, I made a batch of banana pancakes. I'm the third-string chef at our house, so after a few minutes our kitchen was beginning to look like a flaming Kuwaiti oil field.

As I was cooking, I turned to the boys gathered at the table and asked, "Who wants to pray for all this?" The kid who hadn't been to church quickly volunteered. I turned around, smiled, and said, "Go for it."

We all reverently bowed our heads. We waited in silence. We waited in more silence. That was followed by more silence.

"Uh, Tony, are you going to pray?" I asked.

He looked up at me and whispered, "I'm not sure if I should pray for the pancakes or us!"

Jesus prayed a lot, and he encouraged others to do the same. He introduced people to a kind of prayer they had never encountered before. He demonstrated that God wishes a lively, one-to-one connection with us. It is through that conduit that God acts.

Keep it brief; keep it alive.

I'm often asked by professionals why people should pray. It's a good question. Jesus clearly demonstrated that amazing events are set in motion when individuals take it upon themselves to ask God for help. You needn't have a prayer meeting in the boardroom to accomplish this. Rather, in quiet or down times give conscious thanks for your career, ask for wisdom in dealing with irritable partners, and seek patience in handling troublesome customers. Keep it brief, and keep it alive. I suggest you hold your breath; prayers seem to make things happen.

46

Write in the Dirt

A subtle element of Jesus' relationship skill wasn't often reported, but it demonstrated how to act under pressure. He held a clinic on it when the religious leaders brought him a woman caught in the act of adultery. Unlike the other kangaroo court questions they invented to trap him, it was a real-life dilemma. The woman would be killed by stoning or spared based upon their judgment alone.

The fact that they brought her to Jesus is itself amazing and probably underscores their simmering frustration with having no clear grounds upon which to discredit him. The air pulsed with their bittersweet delight in finally being able to checkmate the troublesome whelp.

We know that Jesus had a commanding presence, but here we see a man possessed of uncanny coolness and deliberation. The hotter the situation grew, the more relaxed he became. He had been teaching a crowd when the Pharisees broke in, so he had not only hostile authorities but also an audience to deal with. How did he reply to the pressured and potentially disastrous situation?

There is no need to be forced;
be deliberate.

He crouched down and began writing in the dirt.

When was the last time you were put on the hot seat? Did you quiver and blush? Did you stammer and squirm? Did you feel defensive and unsure? Can you feel the urgency for Jesus to respond quickly?

The Pharisees grew impatient and demanded an answer. Jesus finally stood up and said, "All right, go ahead. Stone her. Let the person who has never sinned throw the first stone" (John 8:3–11, paraphrase). Then he crouched down again and continued writing.

The crowd of perpetrators fell silent, and the audience dispersed, age before youth. It grew quiet after a while. Jesus looked up and realized that just he and the woman remained in the temple yard.

"Where are your accusers? Didn't they condemn you?" Jesus asked.

"No, Lord," she replied.

"Neither do I. Go and sin no more."

We're astonished at such wisdom. I doubt that even the wisest among us could render such simple brilliance on the spur of his or her best moment.

Sometime today you'll be placed in a hot spot. Maintain your composure, and avoid thoughtless, knee-jerk comments. Facing a tough decision, you should feel free to crouch down and write in the dirt until you hear God's wisdom. There is no rush, no matter how hard your cohorts or superiors press you to talk.

47

Know Your Worst Defector

I t's time to talk about the most infamous snitch of all, Judas Iscariot. Judas certainly had all the qualities of an "inner circle" person. There is no reason to think Judas had foreknowledge that he would betray his teacher in the end. But Judas did know that he was a double-minded person, capable of acting like a die-hard brother but in fact being perfectly willing to bail out. Jesus knew it all, yet kept his identity secret from the others.

Conventional wisdom begs to ask why Jesus didn't root him out. A larger question is, Why did Jesus knowingly allow him inside to begin with? These are good questions to answer, because like Jesus, you have a defector in your life. Jesus knows that person and has prepared a lesson for him or her in advance.

Jesus understood that his main task on earth was to create followers with hearts indivisibly devoted to God. He knew that a little religion could carry most people through their everyday trials, but enduring the wrenching destined for those who followed him would be the ultimate test of sincerity. Hypocrites can survive the calm times with hardly a mussed

> *We know Judas better than we think we do.*

hair. But rough times and calamities test what's deepest in a person.

I wonder at times if Jesus didn't intend on using Judas as a mirror for us all to look at ourselves. Perhaps instead of casting aspersions on Judas, we should admit that to some extent we're just like him. We are not always 100 percent devoted to our own agendas, our own people, our own plans. We're capable of duplicity and desertion, hypocrisy and laziness.

Sometimes just admitting it is the first step to righting it. Wherever your relationships are serious business, you must make a daily recommitment to truth and loyalty. Relationships built on sporadic effort and feeble commitments will fail. Rather be of clear purpose, fully devoted to scaling higher mountains of involvement with your people regardless of cost. That's about as far away from Judas as you can get.

48

Apply Uncommon Wisdom

An eight-year-old boy named Hank lives across the street from me. I really like this kid; he is bright as a new penny and gutsy. He loves to talk, and he is a bottomless source of hilarious and at times vexing childhood wisdom.

Not long ago Hank and I were talking on our front porch. The topic of girls came up, and his eyes began to sparkle.

He said, "Did you know that [your son] Jake went on a date last year?"

My body instinctively leaned forward in surprise, hanging nervously on his comment.

"Excuse me?" I gagged.

"Yeah. He met a girl at the movies, and they had a date," he said.

My first thought was, *Define "date,"* but instead I said, "He didn't even tell me!"

I choked out a short laugh, and I must have stopped smiling.

Hank was quiet for several seconds, realizing that he had said too much. It was a long, tense moment as we both

---

*If it sounds common, don't say it;
if it is common, don't think it.*

thought hard and fast. Suddenly his expression signaled he had found a way out of his precarious mess.

"Mr. Beausay, I think Jake is afraid to expose his real *outer* self to you. Maybe you should listen to Dr. James Dobson. It would help you understand Jake better."

An eight-year-old!

Jesus was a fountain of uncommon wisdom. Consider this paraphrased list:

- "I came not to cure the healthy, but to cure the sick" (Matt. 9:12).
- "The first will be last, and the last will be first" (Matt. 19:30).
- "I say to forgive people up to seventy times seven" (Matt. 18:22).
- "Blessed are the poor, the meek, and the down-trodden, for they shall inherit the kingdom of God" (Matt. 5:3ff.).
- "I am the way, the truth, and the life; nobody can come to the Father but through me" (John 14:6).

And many more. These truths were so wise and so completely unexpected that silence was the only reasonable reply.

Uncommon wisdom is mined out of unusual sources. Look and listen for these sources. Perhaps they will be janitors, secretaries, retired neighbors, or bus drivers. Develop skepticism about people who spout common thinking, and be ears up for uncommon wisdom. Commit yourself to pushing your experience forward by occasionally thinking against the grain of the crowd.

49

Keep Your Friends Informed

Sir Arthur Conan Doyle once played a practical gag on his three best friends. He anonymously sent each a telegram that simply said, "All has been found out."

By that very evening, all three had left town.

Faith Popcorn, in her marvelous little book entitled *The Popcorn Report,* identifies a social trend she claims will define the American family and business life in the next generation. She calls this trend *cocooning.* Cocooning involves people withdrawing into the privacy and safe sanctuary of their homes or offices, being preoccupied with electronic toys and essentially insulating themselves against a world they neither understand nor feel able to control.

We're seeing this already. There are increasing pressures on us to keep people out of our lives rather than let them in. Think of work where closed cubicles and E-mail keep people out of one another's way and ostensibly more productive. We hesitate to talk about ourselves should some skeleton from our lives escape into open daylight! We sense it at home, too, in our quiet, intense preoccupation with the new national pastime: computers and the Internet. We're evolving into a nation

Find someone you trust and tell all.

of hiders, deftly wielding smoke and mirrors to keep others away at any cost.

We cannot hide our weaknesses and mistakes forever. Hiding, decoying, and cocooning are relational suicide.

Jesus made every effort to strip the cocoon off his life. As the pressure mounted in Jesus' final years, he kept his friends closely informed. He told them everything. He repeatedly mentioned the humiliations and troubles he would face. None of his twelve disciples really understood what he was talking about, but that didn't stop Jesus from sharing all the gruesome details. He hid nothing.

Keeping our friends informed requires high priority, as well as a great deal of faith. Following the lead of Jesus, keep your closest friends informed. Let them in, no matter how humiliating or difficult your situation becomes. Share the truth, seek input, ask for help, and make them a part of your team. It's hard, but it's distinctly human.

50

Less Is More

I know a very wealthy man who gives away cash donations on holidays. He gives cash to several local charities to disperse as they see fit. Over the years, his generosity has meant a warm Thanksgiving and Christmas for thousands of families.

As chance would have it, I was present one year when the people from the charity arrived to pick up a check. Two older women shuffled through the door of the office and were met immediately by the receptionist. Both women looked homeless. Their warmth and good cheer, however, were unmistakable.

The receptionist asked them to be seated while a check was drawn for them. They talked quietly and chuckled a bit to themselves, smiling often. I couldn't miss the irony that the two bag ladies, haggard and poor, were the ones really giving something on the holiday. The contrast between rich and poor was clearly drawn for me.

It was made clearer when my friend emerged from his office to sign the check. He was having a bad day; his face was stained by a dark shadow of rage he only halfheartedly hid

---

*Discover what you have,
then give it away.*

from the tattered little angels. He signed the check and quickly returned to his office, directing me to follow.

I would have preferred to stay with the women. You should have seen their twinkly faces! They held that check as if it was a napkin autographed by Lawrence Welk. Wide-eyed and smiling, they thanked the receptionist repeatedly and turned happily toward the door. My grumpy friend turned back toward me and sarcastically fumed, "I hope that makes them happier than it made me."

Jesus encountered odd attitudes about charity and used them to teach a valuable lesson about relationships. He was once perched over a crowd in the temple watching rich people flaunting their public tithes. His disciples were standing close by when Jesus suddenly hailed them over. He was pointing at a diminutive older bag lady. She was a widow, the poorest of the poor. Into the coffers she put a measly two pennies (Luke 21:1ff.).

"She has given more than anyone," Jesus said, "because she has given everything she had."

In relationships, give what you have. Don't skimp. You are rich in relational currency. You cannot expect to give a tiny portion of your wealth and get much back. Rather, give all you have. Be gracious with your time and input, and your relationships will blossom correspondingly.

51

Antifear

J esus never talked much about fear. That is surprising given that fear was as predominant an emotion then as it is now. Eyewitnesses often reported that the people approaching Jesus were consumed by fear, yet he never mentioned it, choosing instead to puncture it with his actions.

How he did that is vital for those of us wishing to handle the fears that choke work and home life. First, we must understand the antithesis of fear from Jesus' perspective.

Ask your coworkers or professional peers to define the opposite of fear and you'll hear answers such as "courage," "toughness," and "hope." From battle-hardened people like us, these definitions make sense.

Jesus had a completely fresh and novel perspective. He demonstrated its potence over and over again. I'll tell you what *antifear* is if you promise not to roll your eyes.

Antifear is love.

I asked you not to roll your eyes because we have become too cynical about this overused and underpracticed tool. Love is not a soft, bouncy breeze that whisks away fear; love is a serrated, diamond-hard, double-edged, poison-tipped harpoon

---

Be a fear piercer.

capable of instantly annihilating fear. It plunges deeply, eliminating fear and its bitter children, anxiety and worry.

Jesus demonstrated love on many occasions. One involved an unusual overlapping of two people and their terrifying problems. Jesus had been begged to visit the dying daughter of a temple leader named Jairus. On his way through the crowds with his disciples and Jairus, a desperately ill and poor woman reached out and touched Jesus. She was immediately healed.

Jesus felt power leave him, whirled around, and asked "whodunit" questions. Put yourself in the woman's shoes. She was horrified by what she had done. In front of the whole crowd she made a quivering, sobbing confession. Midway through her mercy pleas, Jesus pierced her fear with the most loving words she had probably ever heard: "Daughter, your faith has made you well. Go in peace" (Mark 5:34).

As he was speaking, a messenger approached Jairus with the news that his daughter was dead. Only moments before he had been prostrate at Jesus' feet, fearfully begging for her life. We can only imagine what he was feeling the moment the bad news arrived.

Without a pause, Jesus cut to the heart of his fear with the antidote: "Don't be afraid! Trust in me and she'll be all right."

She was.

It's much easier to use this tool than you may think. Since fear resides in each person you'll encounter today, invest a few short seconds and pierce it with love, and salve it with a kind word. It will mean a great deal to them and give you back more than you'll immediately recognize.

52

What's Really Important?

I t was totally unfair. Jesus was visiting Mary and Martha's place for dinner. Martha had been cleaning and preparing the house all day. She fixed dinner, set the table, made all the numerous arrangements, and had still more to do. Her lazy sister Mary could have at least offered to lift a finger to help (Luke 10:38ff.).

But no! She spent all her time sitting with rapt attention at Jesus' feet in the living room, hanging on every word he spoke. Finally Martha could take no more.

"Don't you think it's just a little unfair that my sister sits here while I do all the work?" she blurted out.

Not missing the chance, Jesus turned to Martha and offered some insightful words.

"Martha, Martha, why are you so upset over these details? There is really only one detail that matters, and Mary has found it," Jesus said.

Maybe it's time to reassess what's really important in your life. In all of our professional and private pursuits, we attempt to gain efficiency and leverage by properly aligning our priorities. But we often fail to periodically reassess these priorities to check if they are still relevant, necessary, or even

What looks important often isn't.

helpful. Priorities that begin as helps often end up being curses.

Jesus was very comfortable helping people realign the priorities that drove both their anxieties and their effectiveness. He was quick to help them put their energies toward something more vital than table settings and insignificant protocol.

53

Walking Dead People

An anonymous quote is written atop my mission statement. It says, "We act as though comfort and luxury were the chief ingredients of happiness, when all we really wanted was something to be excited about."

Nine out of ten people you meet today are walking dead people. They don't really know what it means to feel excitement, to have a glistening hope, a dream, or a passion. They have traded it all.

This statement may strike you as heresy, but Jesus didn't come to make people good. He came to bring people to life. It was a key skill he used with nearly everyone he met.

Jesus was hounded by the comfort and luxury seekers. He often gave them what they sought, then suggested what they should really strive for was something slightly more valuable.

A notable example is the healing of a man born blind. Later when he and Jesus met publicly, Jesus told him that his purpose was not only to give sight to the blind, but also to see that people might have life more fully.

Every day is a new chance to live.

This is a perplexing statement given our current situation of walking death. Our careers are choking us with work groups, competition, lawsuits, work reviews, lack of teamwork, jealousy, politics, and more. "More abundant life" sounds pretty good right now.

The shortest route to it is what Jesus did. Fix yourself on doing the daily routines that are required, but resist becoming a part of them. Always keep your eye fixed on bringing more life to the routines rather than the routines bringing more emptiness to you.

54

Listening

Not long ago my sons found an old bow and arrow set in our garage. They rushed into the backyard with wild plans to see what they could hit. Visions of becoming Olympic archers whizzed cleanly through their minds.

They wasted no time setting up a target. Their breathlessness frightened me, so I decided to give a quick physics lesson.

Too late.

Have you ever heard of Zachary's corollary to Newton's first law of inertia? It states that if your aim stinks, expect your arrow to fly onward past the target and "thwaaaccckkk" into the side of the house. That usually leads to Bill's corollary to Newton's second law, which is related to volcanic explosions. You get the idea.

My boys came to me hardened with adolescent theories and ignorant explanations for what happened. The hand of God must have gripped my throat because I could not speak. I just listened. The more they talked, the more I listened, sans explosions, threats, and tirades. They were probably as

---

Ears up; ears on.

surprised by my silence as I was, and their hearts quickly softened into teachable lumps.

I was shocked at what I was hearing. As I listened, they admitted they erred and offered to fix the problem and aim better in the future. I didn't need antacids, and they didn't need earplugs or books to read while they served their sentences. I was awed by the results of a little divinely imposed listening.

Few of us listen well. One of the frailties of humanity is the mistaken belief that what we have to say is more important than what we have to hear. When we close our ears, our minds shut as well. Not only is communication lost, but so are sensitivity and responsiveness. Both are crucial elements in any success formula.

The chief reason people abandoned Jesus was that they had hearts hardened by lack of understanding. Jesus cleverly handled that by listening carefully. He won many hearts by not following Bill's corollary. He could have preached and ranted and screamed. Rather, Jesus patiently listened to what people had to say, then responded directly to their words, often expanding on their logic. Listening isn't that hard to do. What's difficult is making the decision to try.

55

Please Go Away

I heard a professional football coach com-plaining about his players on the opening day of training camp. He said, "I have one hundred players in camp, and I have one hundred problems, all of which have nothing to do with football."

We all have big problems that have little to do with the work we must complete or career we must build. The weight of the world crushes hearts all around us right now. And these people will never say anything about it.

Think about your job. Think about the immense number of lives that intersect there, countless life stories intertwined for eight hours, mixing and matching in incalculable ways. For the most part, these stories are painful, sorrowful, anxious, nervous, heart twisting, and more. And not one of them has anything to do with work.

It's no wonder coworkers often want everyone to stay clear. They hurt and feel so badly about themselves that they cannot bear to be in the presence of anyone.

That happened once to the apostle Peter, a professional fisherman. Jesus had told Peter to put out his nets to catch some fish, and Peter scoffed, telling Jesus that he had already

How can I help?

been out fishing and nothing was biting. Jesus told him to just do it, and when he did, the catch was so large, Peter's net tore (Luke 5:6ff.).

Humiliated, Peter fell to the ground and begged Jesus to leave him, a miserable, faithless loser.

"Don't be afraid," Jesus reassured. "I'll make you a fisher of men." Jesus knew that there was no need to carry the burden of heartache and guilt alone.

We can all learn a basic lesson from this story. Recognize the anguish in other people's actions, and offer a lifeline. Ask them how you can help, and tell them you're available. They won't always take it, but inside they'll be grateful for your effort. On a relational level, it's a profoundly powerful gesture. Such kindness builds connections with huge payoffs both at work and at home.

56

Ask for What You Want

J esus demonstrated a gift of being able to ask people directly for what he wanted. A remarkable example was his interaction with a corrupt and hated local politician named Zacchaeus (Luke 19:2ff.).

Zacchaeus desperately wanted to see Jesus. He had never seen him before, and in order to get a glimpse he raced ahead of the crowd and climbed a sycamore tree. Soon the entourage came past the tree, and Zacchaeus got a bird's-eye answer to his wish.

Little did he know he was to play a starring role in the traveling drama. As Jesus passed, he looked upward at Zacchaeus and made a direct statement: "Come down here now, Zacchaeus. I'm staying at your house tonight!"

A stunned Zacchaeus froze, no doubt wondering how the prophet knew him. He quickly climbed down from the tree and took Jesus to his house.

Few of us are so direct. Social delicacy or perhaps fear constrains us to be more oblique. If you wish more effectiveness in your life, you can easily incorporate a Jesus-style directness and vastly streamline your relationships. Though it can be difficult for you to begin this changeover, people will

---

Tell it straight.

begin to recognize you as a person who deals directly with them.

57

A Disaster Is Always a Step Forward

In the eyes of Mary and Martha, Jesus had dillydallied way too long (John 11:1ff.). It had been many days since they had sent an urgent message asking him to come and heal their sick brother Lazarus. Now he was dead. It was a disaster.

Little did they know, Jesus had tarried on purpose. The purpose was to demonstrate how a disaster is always a step forward for people of faith.

When he arrived, only Martha came to greet him. Her first words were sharp: "If only you had been here, this wouldn't have happened." Mary came shortly after and, falling down at his feet, said, "He wouldn't have died if you had only been here!"

How did Jesus step forward at that moment? The Bible says that Jesus knew what was going to happen. He had seen it all and wasn't going to yield to the demands of the disaster.

Jesus never yielded to the demands of a disaster.

"Where did you put him?" he asked. They escorted him to the tomb, at which time he commanded them to roll the stone aside.

"But he has been dead four days!" they warned him.

"Didn't I tell you that you would see the glory of God if you only believe?" he said.

The steps forward from the disaster were Lazarus's.

We have all known business and personal disasters. What many of us find foreign is the ability to maintain a positive attitude and sense of control during those times. So much of how we will act depends on what we foresee. Our responses to a crisis will vary wildly depending upon whether we see ultimate victory or defeat.

What you foresee depends on your faith. Nourish your faith during tough times, and make yourself see the moments you can step forward. Prepare yourself by looking ahead and readying yourself for the inevitable disasters. Then take the faith-produced steps forward.

58

The Impossible Becomes Highly Probable

All professional athletes make the difficulties of their sports look easy. Pro golfers make hitting out of bunkers look simple. Professional quarterbacks make throwing twenty-yard square outs look like a snap. Professional auto racers make twisting-turning laps at skin-stretching speed look like a Sunday spin in the family sedan. A handspring off a balance beam? Piece of cake.

All accomplished human beings have mastered something difficult to the point of making it look effortless. But admiring the look of excellence and achieving it yourself are two different things.

Jesus and his followers were no different. On one occasion his disciples came to him with a warning that the more than five thousand people in his audience needed to go away and find dinner because it was getting late. Not missing a beat, Jesus replied, "That's not necessary. You feed them" (paraphrase).

> *When Jesus enters, what was previously impossible becomes highly probable.*

I can see their faces. It would be no different from somebody putting boxing gloves on you, then telling you to *just go in the ring and knock out Evander Holyfield.*

Right. Or in the words of the disciples at that moment, "Impossible! All we have is five loaves and two fish" (Mark 6:35ff.).

When Jesus entered a situation, what was previously impossible became highly probable.

"Bring them here, and make the people sit down in the grass," he said just before doing the "impossible" thing of feeding them all.

Jesus reassured us that we could be the kind of people that when we enter a situation, what was previously impossible becomes highly probable. Jesus freely shared with his followers the source of the effortless mastery: "With men this is impossible, but with God all things are possible" (Matt. 19:26).

With patience and instruction Jesus taught that the real source of his miraculous deeds was pure faith, unencumbered by human wisdom or haughty self-reliance.

Pure faith is so easy to use. The problem is that it is so easy *not* to use. Among successful people, nothing is so common as self-reliance. Trading your self-reliance for faith is terribly hard. You have been successful because that's the last thing you do!

Try it. Make a decision to address the impossible situations you face by relying on something greater than yourself. Walk face first into your impossible situations with nothing more than faith in your heart. You won't learn this in B-school, but it's the key to making the impossible highly probable.

59

A Higher Level of Excellence

Jesus never let people stew in past failures; he didn't let them cook in mediocrity; he never let them simmer away in emotional pain. Rather, he boldly and consistently called people to stretch forward to a higher level of living.

Many people in our world dislike real effort, much less stretching themselves hard. Our family members resist being pushed beyond their comfort zones, fellow employees resent anything not included in their job description, friends are angered if challenged about something they believe, and so on. Improving yourself, thinking hard, going above and beyond, challenging yourself, reaching, and the like are not even remotely in vogue.

Though he wasn't always successful, Jesus constantly pressed people higher. Jesus was forward looking when it came to using one's talents. He believed that a person's best days were ahead, and he often tried to stretch people toward their best.

Jesus could often be heard encouraging this stretch with words such as these: "Listen," "Try to understand," "You have heard, but now I say," "Keep on asking," "Follow me now,"

Who knows how high you can go?

"Be of good cheer," "Take heart," and "I am here; don't be afraid!" Those words were clearly not shallow encouragements, but solid ground upon which people could march out of mediocrity.

At one point Jesus really stretched his listeners. In response to a question regarding the Roman "One Mile Law" (local Jews could be forced to carry the Roman military equipment one mile) he provided a shocking admonition to stretch.

"If the Romans ask you to go one mile, go two."

How would your workplace change if today everyone went the second mile? How would your marriage change? Your home life? Your neighborhood? All would be unrecognizable.

Calling people to a higher level of life may cost you friends and support in the short term. It was, however, without question the skill Jesus used to orient people for long-term growth. Feel free to use his words verbatim.